PROCESS-THOUGHT
AND
CHRISTIAN FAITH

PROCESS-THOUGHT
AND
CHRISTIAN FAITH

NORMAN PITTENGER
King's College, Cambridge

The Macmillan Company, New York

Library of Congress Catalog Card Number: 68-8711

FIRST AMERICAN EDITION 1968

First published in Great Britain in 1968 by James Nisbet & Company
Limited

The Macmillan Company, New York
Collier-Macmillan Canada Ltd., Toronto, Ontario

Printed in the United States of America

To

CHARLES HARTSHORNE

Whose many books, ready help,
and deeply Christian spirit
have made it possible for
the author and many others
to retain and deepen their
faith that God is Love

CONTENTS

PREFACE

I must begin with a brief account of my growing appreciation of what in recent years has come to be called process-thought or process-philosophy. As long ago as the late 1920's and early 1930's, a reading of certain Cambridge theologians of the time introduced me to this sort of understanding of human life and the natural world. The work of Professor J. F. Bethune-Baker, Professor Alexander Nairne, Canon Charles Raven, Dr A. C. Bouquet, and the Reverend J. S. Boys-Smith—all of whom were members of an informal group in Cambridge which was developing this line of thought —opened for me the possibility of a re-conception of Christian faith in terms of what was then being described as "emergent evolution". Later in the 1930's when I became a theological teacher, I found the opportunity to read C. Lloyd-Morgan, S. Alexander, Jan Smuts, and above all A. N. Whitehead; it was in those years that I began to work out my own version of this re-statement of the Christian faith. Finally, in the 1940's and thereafter, Charles Hartshorne's books came to be for me the most valuable explication of the process background for my Christian thought.

In 1944, when I published *Christ and Christian Faith*, I was already wrestling with the doctrine of Christ in the light of process-philosophy. Eleven years later in *Theology and Reality* (1955), I sought to apply its concepts to certain other areas of theology; and in the following year, publishing lectures originally given to parish clergy conferences on *Rethinking the Christian Message* (1956), I urged the use of these ideas in the necessary and thorough re-working of the popular presentation of basic Christian themes. My large study in christology, *The Word Incarnate* (1959), was an extended essay in interpretation of the person and work of Jesus in pro-cess-terms. Finally in *The Christian Understanding of Human Nature* (1964) I used process-thought, along with some of the insights of existentialism, the new approach to history, and some of the findings of depth psychology, to elucidate the Christian view of the meaning of manhood.

With this continuing interest and with my enormous respect for what Cambridge theology had been attempting in the years before what Canon Raven called "the great blight" (which followed the exaggerated biblical theology of the 1930's and later years), I was delighted to be asked by the Divinity Faculty of that university to lecture for them in November 1964. My public lecture in that year was followed by other invitations, three in Britain and one in the United States, to give a brief and popular account of process-thought and its importance for Christian theology. The result was the expansion of the original lecture into four lectures which in varying forms were delivered as the Lightfoot Lecture for 1964 at the University of Durham, at the Episcopal Theological College in Edinburgh in 1964, at St Augustine's College, Canterbury in 1965, and as the Beattie Lectures at the University of the South in the United States in April 1966. I thank the authorities of these institutions for their invitations to lecture and for the kind hospitality shown me when I was their guest.

This book might have been, perhaps should have been, much longer and more detailed; and unquestionably it may be faulted as being altogether too much a reporting of what one theologian has found interesting and useful in his study of the process-philosophy. In extenuation I should plead that in a series of four lectures, intended in each instance of delivery for a general educated public rather than for philosophical and theological experts, of necessity one must be brief and must deal with the topic in a broad way; furthermore, I have not intended to claim that every representative of process-thought would agree with what I have selected as significant nor would find my use of what in fact has been selected compatible with his own particular approach or his own individual conclusions. I have not attempted a 'thorough analysis of all the available material but have sought to give a survey which conveys my own impressions of a body of literature that I have studied over many years. Nor should I have published the four lectures had not many who heard them urged that they be made available to a larger public which knew little or nothing about process-thought and its availability for Christian use. My original intention in the lectures and my hope in the publication of this book has been and is that I may stimulate younger colleagues in the theological world to pursue the task with more competence and greater discernment, and perhaps much more radically, than I have been able to do.

In conclusion, I am grateful to Professor D. D. Williams of Union Theological Seminary, New York City, and Professor D. W. Sherburne of Vanderbilt University,

Nashville, Tennessee, for reading the typescript and making many valuable suggestions; and above all to Professor Charles Hartshorne, who has not read the typescript but who, during a recent short visit to England, discussed with me many of the ideas which are found in this book. I have ventured to dedicate to him this introduction to the Christian use of process-thought, as a token of my gratitude for his help and also for the enormous resource that I, with many others, have found in his long years of work in the development of this philosophical conceptuality. Of course none of these persons, but only I, have responsibility for what is said in these pages.

King's College   *Norman Pittenger*
Cambridge

Chapter I

INTRODUCTION

A

A contemporary poet has written of the dilemma of
the modern man who, with his sense of confusion, lack
of meaning in life, and anxiety about the future, comes
to a church service in the hope that something may be
said there which will speak to this condition:

> I come to you in anxiety, and you give me uncertain-
> ties.
> I come without meaning, and you preach nonsense.
> I come in confusion, and you cry "Miracle".
> If my only choice is to be a Christian or a modern
> man,
> I have no choice. Modernity is my name—I am its
> child.[1]

Whatever we may think of the literary quality of this
bit of verse, we can have no doubt that the un-named
writer is expressing a widely felt attitude to the preaching and teaching given by many of those who today
speak for the Christian faith. It may well be that only
the sophisticated—or those who in some lonely moment
have felt what Thoreau called "a quiet sense of despera-
tion"—would wish to say that their condition is properly
described as compounded of anxiety, meaninglessness,

---

[1] Quoted by W. Paul Jones, *The Recovery of Life's Meaning*,
p. 14 (Association Press, New York, 1964).

and confusion. Yet as one reads much that is being written and listens to much that is being said these days, one is more and more inclined to think that some such awareness is much more general among our contemporaries than surface-appearances might indicate. In any event it is plainly the fact that the way in which Christian faith has been and is being presented in many quarters has seemed and does seem to vast numbers of people simply a mixture of uncertainty, nonsense, and "miracle", the last of these in the sense of an appeal sometimes made by Christian apologists and preachers to what strikes the modern man as an absurd and unintelligible violation of the pervasive regularity which he has come to believe is a mark of the universe as he knows it to be. It is also the fact that the choice frequently offered him is between being "a Christian" of a very narrowly "orthodox" type or being "a modern man"; I need cite here only a recent English publication, H. A. Blamires' little book *The Christian Mind*, as a popular, if extreme, expression of this supposed dilemma.

In *Honest to God* the Bishop of Woolwich has said that he himself is *both* a modern man *and* a Christian believer. There is no escaping the former for a man living today, he has rightly told us; and there is no reason why such a man should not also be a Christian. He was entirely correct in saying this, but the difficulty, as Dr Robinson also recognized, is that the way in which all too often we are given to understand Christian faith makes the combination impossible. It is my own belief that the explanation for the enormous sale of *Honest to God* is simply that great numbers of men and women who wish to be both modern and Christian found in that book a presentation of Christianity which on the one hand they felt was absolutely honest and which on the other hand (and for the first time) opened to them the basic meaning of what we may style "the *religious* question": what man is, what his world is like, how one can find significance and dignity for living, and the like. It did this, they thought, in a fashion which was not in outrageous contradiction to everything else that as persons living in the mid-twentieth century they believed to be true.

Dr Robinson relied very largely on the philosophical theology of Paul Tillich for his suggestions about the reconception of Christian faith. There can be no doubt that Dr Tillich was outstanding among the distinguished thinkers of our day who have been working towards a reconception of the faith in the light of contemporary knowledge and contemporary experience. No one, least of all myself (who would acknowledge an enormous debt to Dr Tillich's work and a valued personal friendship with that great and good man), would wish to question his pre-eminence in this field. However, it is my own conviction that there is another kind of thought which is even more suitable for use in the task of Christian reconception. This is the line taken by what in North America today is frequently described as "process-thought"; its greatest exponent was the late Professor Alfred North Whitehead in his works *Process and Reality* (his book has been re-arranged, and provided with excellent explanatory notes by D. W. Sherburne, under the title of *Key to Whitehead's Process and Reality*), *Science and the Modern World*, *Modes of Thought*, *Adventures of Ideas*, *Religion in the Making*, and *Symbolism*, all of them written after Whitehead

had joined the faculty of Harvard University in the
United States in the 1920's.

But Professor Whitehead was only one of a number
of thinkers in the years 1920–35 who were taking the
same general approach to an understanding of man and
his world. Professor C. Lloyd-Morgan's *Emergent Evolution* and *Life, Mind and Spirit*, Professor Samuel
Alexander's *Space-Time and Deity*, General Jan Smuts's
Holism, and other works of a similar nature were appear-
ing during those years. While there were many differences among them, there was also a consistent use of
evolutionary ideas which gave them a genuine unity.
In our own decade, the works of Pierre Teilhard de
Chardin, the noted Jesuit palaeontologist, have been
published posthumously; they too follow the same
general line as the English writers I have mentioned.
Furthermore, in the United States, for over a quarter of
a century the writings of Professor Charles Hartshorne,
including *Beyond Humanism*, *The Vision of God*,
Reality as Social Process, *The Divine Relativity*, *The
Logic of Perfection*, and *A Natural Theology for Our
Times*, as well as many occasional articles and essays,
have eloquently argued the case for "process-thought".
Happily Professor Hartshorne is still at work among us
and further books from his pen may be expected in the
next few years.

None of these books, nor the metaphysical position
which they advocated, has received in recent years the
attention which they deserve in Christian theological
circles. One reason for this has been what Dr H. J.
Paton in *The Modern Predicament* styled "the linguistic veto" on all metaphysical speculation. The linguistic
philosophers, whether in their earlier phase of "logical

positivism" or in their later phase which would confine philosophical enquiry to an examination of "language games" (in Wittgenstein's phrase), have somehow contrived to make the older philosophical task of metaphysical construction appear silly or pretentious— although things are changing today, as may be shown by a remark made to me not long ago by one of the leading British empirical philosophers. This thinker, whose name I shall not disclose, said that he was becoming more and more convinced that there was "something in" the older metaphysical—he called them "ontological"—claims; at the moment he was much concerned, he said, to find a way of giving more than *linguistic* status to such propositions as "personal God", for it appeared to him that these statements somehow pointed to a truth about the universe, about the nature of things, that must be reckoned with in any honest description of the "way things are".

Another reason for the neglect of Whitehead and the other process-thinkers, especially among theologians, has been the long period (from which we now seem to be emerging) when philosophical theology itself, and especially such philosophical theology as employed scientific data as part of its material, was looked upon as a highly dangerous and even sinful intrusion of non-biblical and secular thought into the Christian faith. What some call "biblical theology" has been taken to rule out, once and for all, any such philosophical approach to faith. Not only has it been thought that this is improper; it has been suggested, as I have just noted, that to engage in philosophical theology is even blasphemous or sinful. God has revealed himself either in the pages of Holy Scripture or in the events which the

Bible records; nothing else is needed and anything else diminishes or denies the unique adequacy of biblical revelation. This attitude, which has been widespread in non-Roman and non-Orthodox theological circles, is responsible for the contemptuous dismissal of those theologians (sometimes conveniently tagged "outworn liberals" or "old-fashioned modernists") who attempted in the past or who still attempt in the present to employ in their work the insights of the process-philosophers.

For example, during the twenties and thirties of this century, a group of theologians at Cambridge University was engaged in the task of reconceiving and re-stating Christian faith in the light of what was then called "emergent evolution". I refer to such men as Professor J. F. Bethune-Baker, Professor A. Nairne, Canon C. E. Raven, all of whom are now dead, and Dr J. S. Boys-Smith and Dr A. C. Bouquet, both happily still with us. At the same time Father Lionel Thornton published *The Incarnate Lord* and Dr W. R. Matthews *The Purpost of God* and other books; while in the United States Professor E. W. Lyman produced his great work on *The Meaning and Truth of Religion*, and other writers, far too numerous to mention, were attempting the same task. But for a variety of reasons, not least among them the growing influence of Karl Barth and the continental theologians who at the time were associated with him, this entire effort was rejected in the mid-thirties by a large number of Christian scholars. A sermon preached at that time by Sir Edwyn Hoskyns and later reprinted in *Cambridge Sermons*[1] may perhaps be taken as the symbolic moment of the change. In that sermon Sir

---

[1] *Cambridge Sermons*, pp. 34–35 (Faith Press, London, 1959).

Edwyn remarked in effect that while the Lady Margaret Professor (Dr Bethune-Baker) was urging that the task of theology was to bring about a reconciliation of evolution and faith and to re-state faith in terms congruent with such evolutionary ideas, in his (Hoskyns') opinion the theologian's task was precisely the opposite: it was to show the inadequacy of such ideas and to make clear the incongruity between evolutionary thought and Christian faith.

The recent publication in French, and then in English translation—and this some years after his death—of Teilhard de Chardin's *The Phenomenon of Man* and *The Divine Milieu*, and the avid reading which these and other writings by the same French Jesuit have received, may be said to mark the return in many circles to the possibility of a philosophical theology which is prepared to employ evolutionary motifs. As the publication of Teilhard's work has continued his influence has grown. There are sections in his *The Future of Man*, which is a fascinating collection of papers, essays, and lectures given by Teilhard during the years 1924–50, which clearly point the theme and purpose of the present lectures. For example, Teilhard spoke of the "general and growing state of dissatisfaction in religious affairs"[1] —he was writing in 1949. "For some obscure reason", he wrote, "something has gone wrong between Man and God *as in these days he is represented to Man*". The italics are Teilhard's own; and the succeeding pages of the essay from which the quotation comes show that for him "what has gone wrong" was the failure of much traditional Christian teaching and preaching to see that

[1] P. T. de Chardin: *The Future of Man*, p. 260 (W. Collins, London, 1964).

the *world*—the whole created order in its materiality, along with man's grasp of the importance of secular effort and achievement—is an ongoing movement in which significance is given to human life. Teilhard pointed out that it has been the rejection by many modern men of "an 'extrinsical' God, a *deus ex machina* whose existence can only undermine the dignity of the universe and weaken the springs of human endeavour", which poses Christian thinkers with their problem. He asked if they were prepared to reject such a false conception of the meaning of Deity, not only because the rejection was forced on them by honesty but also because such a "pseudo-God" was a denial of the profound Christian rootage in Incarnation.

It would appear that evolutionary or process motifs are again being forced upon our attention; and Christian thought will neglect them to its own peril. Yet we reiterate that throughout the earlier period in question—from 1935, say, to 1960—a few theologians such as Canon Raven in England had continued along the lines laid down in the twenties, while Professor Hartshorne and some others in the United States (notably E. E. Harris, in such books as *Revelation Through Reason*) were carrying on the work on the strictly philosophical side. Professor Tillich himself, to whom we referred at the beginning of this lecture, although not at all identified with process-thought, was insistent on the necessity for the development of a modern philosophical theology and was increasingly finding himself in sympathy with many of the conclusions of thinkers such as Hartshorne; and more recently, as he himself acknowledged in the preface to the third volume of *Systematic Theology*, he associated his own views with those of Teilhard.

It may be said, I believe, that once more the enterprise of reconception in the light of process-thought is at least a "respectable" one in theological circles. The linguistic and biblicist vetos have been seen to be both arbitrary and unwarranted—which makes it all the more pathetic that Dr Paul van Buren in *The Secular Meaning of the Gospel* still seems to accept them as valid and to rule out "God-statements" as "meaningless" while at the same time his excessive Barthian christocentrism and bibliocentrism turns the patent intention of scriptural statement into a parody of their proper meaning. On the other hand, the work of other younger theologians like Schubert Ogden, in his book *Christ without Myth* and more recently (and admirably) in *The Reality of God,* has shown a way of employing the insights of a soundly based biblical hermeneutic within the context of a specifically process-thought understanding of the human situation and the world in which man's existence is set. Furthermore it is to be noted that through the years that have passed since 1936, Professor Daniel Day Williams, Professor Bernard M. Loomer, and Professor Bernard Meland, all three teaching in the United States, have written extensively in theological journals and occasionally in books, all of them engaging in this same task of employing the main tenets of process-thought for the explication of Christian faith. Professor Williams's recent book entitled *The Spirit and Forms of Love* is a sustained application of the concepts of process-thought to the Christian understanding of love as the cosmic ground and the basic meaning of all existence.

Finally, two or three very recent books may be mentioned which are valuable as attempts to state Christian belief in terms of the conceptuality provided by process-thought: John B. Cobb's *A Christian Natural Theology*, Peter N. Hamilton's *The Living God and the Modern World*, and E. H. Peters' *The Creative Advance*. Professor Cobb has also written another volume, which will be published before the present book appears, in which he explores the historical claims of Christian faith with relation to Whitehead's philosophy; this is entitled *The Structure of Christian Existence*.

The present lectures are intended to present, in brief outline, the main emphases of process-thought as one theologian has understood them and to argue for the use of these emphases in the reconception of Christian faith today. It makes no pretence to be exhaustive; it is at best suggestive, perhaps provocative. If the job is done, and when it is done, much in the commonly understood picture of Christian faith may be altered; but I am convinced that nothing that is centrally important will be lost. A former student of Whitehead's once reported in my hearing that the philosopher himself said, when questioned, that Christian "orthodoxy" could not be reconciled with his philosophy. The meaning of this reported remark depends upon what one understands by "orthodoxy". If one means, as Whitehead seems to have done, a rigid adherence to the letter of past formulations of the Christian faith, what he said is of course true. If one means, however, an insistence on the great affirmations of God as love, God revealed in Christ, God the sustainer of human life and the upholder of man's destiny, then the situation is different.

But it seems to me that we should be wiser if we did not here use the term "orthodoxy" at all; rather, we should speak of the *truth* which Christian faith grasps and by which the Christian believer is grasped. In that case, to repeat, *nothing* will be lost and much will be gained, both for the understanding of the faith in God self-revealed in Christ and for the Church which with all its imperfections and inadequacies has proclaimed this faith to the world through twenty centuries of history.

In any event, the task of reconception is required. Whitehead himself has some telling words about this:

> Those societies which cannot combine reverence for the symbols with freedom of revision, must ultimately decay either from anarchy or from the slow atrophy of a life stifled by useless shadows.[1]

B

What are the assumptions with which process-thought begins? And why should Christian thinkers be interested in process-thought? Here are two preliminary questions to which we should turn before we begin our exposition of the attitude which process-thought in its wider significance takes towards problems such as the nature of deity, the meaning of divine activity in the world, and the nature of man and society.

The first and perhaps the basic assumption of the kind of interpretation of the world which we are here considering, is simply that we are confronted, both in our own human experience and in the description of things with which modern scientific enquiry has made us

[1] A. N. Whitehead: *Symbolism*, p. 88 (Cambridge University Press, 1927).

familiar, with a dynamic rather than with a static reality. Those who take this view would say, for example, that it is absurd to speak of "human nature" as if it were an entity that could be described in categories of substance, if by substance we mean immutable and unchanging *thing*. Man is "on the move"; he is a living, changing, developing creature. If he is to be described at all, the dynamic quality of his existence must be recognized and grasped, even if it is also the fact that through all the changes there are persistent qualities which preserve his identity as human. Likewise the world of nature is not a static affair in which things "continue in one stay"; on the contrary, it is evolving, changing, "in process". Down to the lowest levels of matter, if we may so style them, this capacity for and presence of change and development is to be seen. Indeed Professor Whitehead was prepared to go so far as to say that the electron itself is a "society" or an "organism", marked by movement and dynamic activity. Of course the sense in which such words may be used to describe the various levels in the world will vary according to the particular level which is under consideration at any given time and by any particular science. An electron is not a dynamic society or organism of the same order as an amoeba; certainly it differs vastly from the activity which we note in a living cell, in a plant, in a dog, and *a fortiori* in a man. Yet the world as a whole is *in* process and is *a* process; it is not a finished and settled system composed of discrete entities which are inert, changeless, static.

We are led then to a second assumption which is basic to process-thought. Not only is the world and all that is in it a dynamic movement; it is also an inter-related society of "occasions". Nor is there the possibility of isolating one occasion from another, so that each may be considered in itself alone. On the contrary, it would be a "false abstraction" from the deliverance of experience and of observation to attempt to do this. Into each of the given occasions there enter past events as well as the surrounding and accompanying pressures of other occasions, not to mention the "lure" of the future. To illustrate once again from the area best known to us, this is obvious enough at the human level. A man does not and cannot exist in complete isolation from other men, or from his present environment, or from his own past history and the more general history of the human race of which as man he is a part, or from the natural order to which he and his whole race belong, or from the possible developments which are before him and mankind in general. Each man is a focusing, a con-cretizing, of all these. Thus in being "himself" he is not himself alone; he is all that has gone to make him up, all that surrounds him, all that presses upon him, all that he himself enters into and in which he shares, all which he may be. And that which is true of man, is likewise true in its appropriate way throughout the universe. We live in and we are confronted by a richly inter-connected, inter-related, inter-penetrative series of events, just as we ourselves are such a series of events. Whatever is our own specific identity, it can be asserted of us only when this fact of our sociality, of our organic nature, is grasped and given due emphasis. The same must be said of the world as a whole.

This means that we are not able to make sharp distinctions of an ultimate and definitive kind. We cannot do this between "selves", for (as we have seen) they are inter-penetrating. It also means that in the rich experience which we possess, as we grasp it in that kind of double awareness which Whitehead calls "presentational immediacy" and "causal efficacy", we are given a full and compresent encounter with the world. Hence it is impossible, for instance, to reject the aesthetic and valuational elements in experience, as if these were to be seen as merely "subjective", while the primary qualities of hardness, etc., are taken as genuinely "objective". The fact is that our experience gives us all this together, as being profoundly one in impact upon us; we cannot cut up the world of experience, after the fashion of an earlier philosophy, and speak as if that which in its aesthetic quality has subjective appeal must lack any genuine reality in the world itself, simply because it does not lend itself to a particular kind of analysis by measurement or testing. It is of course true that we can and do make abstractions. We are obliged to make them for practical purposes as well as for a theoretical understanding of this or that special question; but they are exactly what they are called, they are "abstractions" from the richness of experience as we concretely know it.

This many-sided experience as it presents itself to us in its immediacy carries with it the corollary of "causal efficacy". By this, process-thought (as expounded by Whitehead) means that there is given to us, in our experience at all levels (including our "bodily" as well as our intellectual awareness), the sense of a variety of relationships which have played upon us and brought our experience to us in the particular way in which in fact it has been brought. Causation, then, is to be taken as another word for describing the way in which given occasions are brought to a focus and in which they make their impact upon those to whom they are presented. *This* rather than *that* particular occasion is known; we experience *this,* not *that,* possibility. The converging process, whatever it may be, that brings *this* rather than *that* to a focus is a genuine and necessarily given factor which is present in whatever it is that we are experiencing, sensing, feeling, knowing, understanding. What in an older kind of philosophy would have been called the chain-of-cause-and-effect is here seen as being very much richer; it is a congeries of occasions, events, pressures, movements, routes, which come to focus at this or that point, and which for their explanation require some principle that has brought and still is bringing each of them, rather than some other possible occurrence, into this particular concrete moment of what we commonly style "existence".

But what secures such persistence or identity in occasions as we do in fact know, both from observation and from our own experience of ourselves? The answer to this question is given in the concept of the "subjective aim" which is proper to each series of occasions. This aim, which has always about it a directive quality, is to be understood as the goal or end towards which a given process moves, yet it must also be seen as in some sense immanently at work in that process moving it towards its goal or end or actualization. There is an element of teleological concern in all process-thought, whether or not the particular description we have offered is accepted. But this does not mean that each set of occasions is "conscious", in anything like our human sense, of the aim which is before it and which gives it the distinctive identity that it possesses. An acorn is certainly not aware of the "aim" which keeps it moving towards its proper development into an oak-tree. But none the less, what does thus keep it moving towards its proper development is the given subjective aim which is proper to the acorn. And so, in appropriate measure and of course with vast differences at each level, throughout the cosmos. Thus we are delivered from a purely mechanical view of the universe, in which nothing is going on but the re-shuffling of a series of originally given entities. Yet we are not delivered into the hands of the vitalist who would wish to introduce some kind of mysterious psyche or entelechy or spirit (or whatever equivalent term he might use) as an *addition* to the process. God himself is possessed of a subjective aim; and every entity in the process, understood as dynamic, inter-related, inter-penetrative of every other entity (and hence better described as an occasion or instance along some "route"), is also characterized by such an aim. This is a truly organic and hence integrative view of "the way things go".

Finally, because of the nature of the world as we know it, we cannot grasp it with that kind of absolute clarity which a Cartesian type of thinking would demand. Indeed we must always seek clarity, as Whitehead once said; but he went on to say that at the same time we must always distrust it. For the difficulty is that simple explanations, which tend always to assume an omnicompetent knowledge, are likely to give us *falsely* simple explanations. If we accept experience as we know it, there will be some things which will appear relatively clear, but they will be set in contexts which are not so clear. Hence the picture of truth is much more that of a small area of fairly straightforward knowledge which shades out into more and more mysterious and unclear knowledge or intimation or hint or apprehension, than it is that of "clear and distinct ideas" which leave no room for doubt and presume to give a simple and direct explanation of any given moment of experience.

A consequence of these assumptions is the rejection of all those dualisms which would make simple divisions or disjunctions between subjective and objective, between man and his world, between mind and matter, between natural and supernatural, and the like. This is *one* world, however diversified it may be; it is all held together in the kind of unity which we know in ourselves—as beings who are not "souls" or "minds" inhabiting "bodies", but who ourselves are the rich unity of all those ranges of experience with which we are familiar, so that (if this kind of language is permissible at all) we must recognize that we *are* minds and we *are* bodies—or better, we are *ourselves* as we know ourselves in the uncomplicated immediacy of our experience of ourselves as being precisely *ourselves* and not something other or less.

A concluding comment may be appropriate here in respect to our first question. The use of human language is for process-thinkers not restricted to the games we play with words. On the contrary, there is for them a more "realistic" insistence on the use of language as being of necessity the symbols for that which we experience or observe. Of course words are arbitrary in one sense, for other terms and other languages are possible. But in another sense they point towards and alone make possible some grasp of that which is really there to be known. They are not empty sounds but have acquired and now convey meanings; they possess an evocative and denotative quality. Inadequate as they are, subject to modification from time to time, needing correction and supplementation, our various human languages (verbal and pictorial, aural or graphic) are both necessary for us and useful to us; they help to make sense of, and they help to give sense to, the richness of experience and the given-ness of the world as we observe and grasp it. Man is a symbol-making and symbol-using animal, but his symbols are not merely subjective. The activity of symbolization is part of his equipment for understanding himself and his world. It is possible therefore —and it is entirely legitimate—to engage in the metaphysical enterprise with the use of such languages as we possess. To refuse to engage in this enterprise, or to reject it as an impossibility, is equivalent to denying to man any capacity to understand who and what he is and what his experience tells him about the world in which he lives.

Our second preliminary question concerned the reason or reasons why Christian thinkers should be interested in process-thought. An approach to an answer may be found by mention of a particular insistence found in one way or another in all the thinkers of this school. Professor Whitehead has used the term "importance" to describe this insight, but there are many other possible ways in which it may be stated and other process-thinkers have their own terms to describe it. But using Whitehead's word, we may say that "importance" is appropriately employed to indicate the fact that some specific occurrence, some particular event or series of concrescent events, some particular stance or attitude, provides for any responsible thinker the "clue" which he takes for his understanding of "how things go". For example, we are all aware of the way in which a moment in the life of a man which to him seems to have decisive importance will give him his criterion of interpretation for all that happens to him. Some historical event, as we well know, can have a determinative significance for our comprehension of a whole series of preceding and succeeding historical events. That which in this sense is "important" not only seems to sum up or to crystallize (so to say) our prior experience, but also opens up for us new avenues of possibility, leading to future interpretations which will be enriching and deepening in our experience. Even more significant, the "important" will actually inaugurate a new level of understanding and thus give rise to a new level of experience for us and for those who follow us. It has an objective as well as a subjective quality. To this concept of "importance" we shall return in other contexts. At the moment it is helpful in our endeavour to see why process-thought has interest for Christian theology.

The point is of course obvious. The Christian believes that in the events of which Scripture is the record, and supremely in the events which find their focus in the life and activity of Jesus Christ, there is a disclosure of something which in the highest degree is "important". Since the Christian is convinced that this is the case, a kind of philosophy which is congruous with such a conviction should be very welcome indeed. Furthermore, if it can be shown that there are many points in which the Christian conviction of what is "important" is illuminated by such a philosophy, the Christian will inevitably have more than academic interest in the way in which that philosophy interprets the world and human experience.

Many of us are certain that this relationship of congruity and illumination which we have noted in respect to the concept of "importance" is true also between many other assertions of Christian faith and the conclusions of process-thought. Of course to say this is also to say we are certain that the biblical narrative and witness demand a metaphysical interpretation. In other words, it is to say that we believe that implicit in the pictorial language of the Scriptures and the historical events to which the Bible points and with which its language is concerned, there is a basic view of the world which is grounded in reality itself. It is obvious that the Hebrew mind did not think about and certainly did not handle this view in conceptual terms such as the Greeks, for example, were ready to employ in their philosophy. But despite the assertions of certain biblical scholars, this does not mean that no metaphysic is implicit in Hebrew thinking; it means only that the language in which the implicit metaphysic was stated was for the Hebrew highly imaginistic, pictorial, symbolical. The Hebrew mind, as represented in the Scriptures, did its thinking in a metaphorical fashion; indeed it might be said that the Jews thought mythologically, if by this word we mean that they thought in pictures and in stories, rather than in abstract concepts and Greek philosophical ideas. But they *thought*.

Granted this difference, it would seem that there is a remarkable correspondence between the biblical insistence on the living God who is active in nature and in the affairs of men, and the recognition by process-thought that the world is a dynamic process of such a kind that whatever explanatory principle or agency there may be must be of that sort too—it also must be dynamic and processive. The Jewish-Christian tradition has never really been content with an "unmoved mover" as the final principle of explanation, however often the notion has been found in classical theologies. It has been uneasy when the God about whom it talks is described in substantial terms of a kind which leave little room for his boundless energizing activity in the world; it has been obliged to seek all sorts of verbal devices for putting life into such language. Process-thought in fact is much closer to the biblical way of seeing things, with its recognition of the profound importance of activity, movement, and development.

Furthermore, the whole creation itself, both what we call nature and also the realm of historical happening, is for the biblical writers open at every point to the action of the living God. They do not see it as a fixed entity, already made and finished; for them the creation is a directed movement in which novelty occurs, in which the unexpected may and indeed often does happen, and in which great ends are in process of achievement. A view of the world which regards it as a finished product has little relation to the world as the Bible sees it; while a world that is nothing but a complicated mechanism, like a machine which grinds along engaged in nothing but repeating standard patterns of behaviour, is not the world of movement and change of which the Scriptures speak. The Bible tells us of a *faithful* God whose purpose is unchanging; hence whatever he does will be consistent with his ultimate objective, while the created world will not be the scene of irrelevant and meaningless intrusions. But with all his faithfulness God is living and active, and the creation is not a "finished" world, much less a dead and inert substance. Granted once again that the biblical witness is in highly pictorial terms and that its "science" is outmoded, the fact yet remains that the biblical witness is to what we have styled an "open" world in which new things occur; that biblical witness always recognized the possibility of novel as well as significant developments.

Once again, the insistence of process-thought on inter-relationship as basic to the world should be welcome to Christian theologians. The great biblical affirmations about God are always made with reference to "God-and-his-world". Whatever is said in Scripture about "God-in-himself" is always to be understood as inference from what is known of his activity in creation. And if he is indeed, what the Christian believes him to be, a loving as well as a living God, then it is obvious that he cannot be seen in abstraction from the world which he loves; for love signifies relationship, and the richest perfection possible is perfection in relationships and not "absolute power" or unchanging substance. An approach to the world and God in terms of process-thought can bring one very close to the Christian conviction that God is genuinely, not simply verbally, describable as "love"—and as love which participates, shares, and even suffers.

The emphasis (to which we shall turn later) of process-thinkers on what Whitehead called the "consequent nature" of God—that is to say, on God's being affected by and actually enriched in his activity by that which occurs in his world—can provide some "secular" confirmation for the Christian's conviction that God not only "cares" for the creation but also finds satisfaction in his world. As Hartshorne has insisted, God is not made *more* divine by that satisfaction, but his deity is given a real enhancement and a genuine delight by what happens in creation; furthermore, the implementation of his purposes is made fuller by these happenings. In other words, the creation *matters* to him. Contrariwise, failures in the creation and a turning-away from its purpose of augmented good are equally real to God, although in the ongoing process he is able to absorb them into himself and to make them serve his ends in ways which would not otherwise be available.

All this should be of interest to the Christian thinker, for it enables him to find (as we have said) a "secular" confirmation for his belief in the God whose suffering love shares in the world's pain while at the same time his triumphant joy is in part derived from the happiness which the world can know. The reality of evil and of good, of pain and of joy, is recognized. But it is seen in relationship to the basic activity which is God himself who is able both to bring good out of evil and at the same time to rejoice in the good which is achieved in the creation. God is vulnerable and shares the world's pain, yet he can use evil (once it has occurred) to accomplish good. The Cross, in itself an "evil" thing, was used by God; and Christians believe it was used by him to bring about greater good than would have been possible without it. If at this point they go *beyond* process-thought, they do not *contradict* its insight.

Again, the insistence on the societal nature of the world, and on man's genuine participation since he himself is organic to that world, illuminates the Christian belief that man belongs to the creation and that the whole natural order, as well as human history and personal experience, is integral to the purpose of God. This applies both to creation and to redemption. A false spirituality which would try to remove man from his material and embodied situation and regard him as an "angel" is seen for the blatant absurdity which it is; on the other hand, the attempt to think that God purposes to "save" man *out of* the world is seen to be a denial not only of the Christian gospel but of a sound understanding of human nature. Man is a body, as he is a mind and a spirit. He is, in fact, *man*; and as man he is a developing unity in relationship with his fellows, with history, and with nature. Therefore what happens in society, in the historical process, and in the natural order of events, has significance for him, because he is participant in this total pattern. God deals with him in *this* fashion, not as if he were an isolated "soul".

Finally, the stress of process-thought on experience, and the richness of "presentational immediacy" coupled with "causal efficacy", should interest the Christian because it demonstrates that in what nowadays it is fashionable to call "meeting", participation in life, and genuine acquaintance by sharing, we come to the fullest knowledge both of ourselves and others and also of the world and God. God is not "up there" or "out there". He is *here*, in the immediacy of our experience; and it is here that he is to be known, obeyed, and adored.

Whatever may be said about transcendence must be said with all this in view. The transcendence of God is his inexhaustibility, not his remoteness. He is richer and fuller in his life than any awareness of him which is possible for us, yet he is not far off but close at hand. He is the "depth" of things, as he is the "depth" of ourselves; but he is more than that—he is *himself*, yet always himself in relation to that which he is doing, loving, using for the world whose final explanation he is. Even when he is not recognized under some conventional name—even when he is not "named" at all—he is the inescapable energy which moves through all things and which works in all things for the richest possible good. Hence men do not need to be introduced to him as if they had never met him; what they need is to identify him where he is, to recognize him as being what he is, and to see him as doing what he does—which, in Christian faith, is to see him as the dynamic, living, loving "Father of our Lord Jesus Christ".

I have not exhausted, by any means, the reasons for a Christian interest in process-thought. But I hope that I have indicated a *few* of the reasons and thus have prepared the readers for the consideration of some of the main emphases in process-thought as they have relevance for the task of Christian reconception.

Chapter II

GOD AND THE DIVINE ACTIVITY
IN THE WORLD

A

In his Gifford lectures, *Process and Reality,* Professor Whitehead wrote the following words: "God is not to be treated as an exception to all metaphysical principles to save their collapse. He is their chief exemplification."[1]

These words provide an excellent starting-place for a consideration of the concept of God which is to be found in process-thought. First they make it clear that what Whitehead in another place referred to as "paying God metaphysical compliments" is for this sort of philosophy a basic error of method. Rather, the task is to find the necessary principles for making sense of the world, while at the same time it is clear that any principles which properly can be said to make sense of things will be those which are not in stark contradiction of all that realm of which, in fact, sense is being made. If the world is a world in dynamic movement, then God as its chief principle of explanation will himself be in dynamic movement; if ceaseless adaptation to novel possibilities is found in the order of creation, the meaning of creation will itself include a factor which in the highest degree is adaptable. For sound explanation it is essential that we look for genuine congruity between God and his world,

[1] A. N. Whitehead: *Process and Reality,* p. 521 (Cambridge University Press, 1927–28).

rather than that we attempt to find ways in which God can be removed from all contact with and reflection in that world and hence treated as nothing other than the great "exception".

A consequence of this approach is that for process-thought deity is not understood as characterized chiefly by "aseity", as if God could be said to "exist" without the continuing relationships and the ceaseless activity which in another way we see reflected in the world which we observe. It has indeed been a strange perversion of the theological mind to employ for our picture of God the "model" which we find most reprehensible when we see it in human form. A man who is utterly self-contained and whose chief ambition is to be "self-existent" and hence to exist without dependence upon relationships of any sort, is a man whom we regard as an unpleasant if not vicious specimen of the race; and it is odd that deity has been regarded, and this even in Christian circles, as more like such a self-contained human being rather than as like a man who in every area of his life is open to relationships and whose very existence is rich in the possibility of endless adaptations to new circumstances.

Recognition of the need for an interpenetrative societal view of the world, perhaps more than any specific *philosophical* requirement, has led process-thinkers to place their emphasis upon "becoming", as a dynamic movement of development in relationship, rather than upon "being"; here, they insist, is the best "model" for our understanding of God. This is not to say that there is no sense in which God "is". His self-identity, established by his "subjective aim" or purpose of self-realization in all his relationships, is always the same: *he is*

God. But if the world provides any clue to the nature of deity, for God to *be* God must imply vital actuality and ceaseless capacity for adaptation; and this may properly be said to define deity as "living" and not as a static entity.

If this way of thinking is correct, it follows that God is not "abstract" but is richly "concrete". This divine concreteness is at least in part derived from his participation in the world itself, whose processive nature he both explains and supremely exemplifies in his own processive nature. There is a considerable variety in the ways in which process-thinkers have attempted to state this position. The way which we shall follow here is largely that of Whitehead and Hartshorne, since this seems the most consistent and coherent. Let us begin by noting that the reason there *must* be deity is that there must be some reason why things are as they are and why they "go" as they "go". Among all the possibilities which are open in the total scheme of things, there must be a reason why the particular actual achievements which we know to be there are in fact present. God is taken to be that principle which will explain why *this* rather than *that* set of possibilities for good has been actualized in the world we experience and observe. He is "the principle of concretion" who by his "decision" has established the good which is in the order of things as it is. As "primordial"—abstract and in this sense "eternal"— God may be said to "contain" all that might ever be. But among all the possibilities of "whatever might be", certain specific occasions do in fact come to be. It is to explain this concrete world, with its emergent order and value, that the concept of God is required metaphysically.

Yet it is also true to say that what comes to be has its consequences in creating new possibilities for what may happen hereafter. As a process, the future is based upon the past; what has happened and what does happen determines, in a general way, what is *to* happen. If God be the supreme exemplification rather than the contradiction of metaphysical principles required to explain the world, then it can be said that what happens enters into the continuing decisions which are made by deity for the establishment of further actualities. In his "consequent" nature, which is as real as but much more concrete and specific than his "primordial" aspect, God is affected by that which occurs in the created order, for what happens enters into his life and influences his "decision" by providing new possibilities for his further activity. While he always remains *God* as the chief principle of explanation for such concrete emergents of the good—in all its variety—as do in fact appear, he is "enriched" both by satisfaction in what happens and by the provision of possibilities of future action by that which has happened.

Therefore time—or succession as the world exemplifies it—is real to God. He is not above and outside all temporality, in an eternity which negates succession; rather temporality is both a reflection of his own dynamic life and also enters into his own reality. *What happens matters to God*. And it matters to him in more than a superficial sense, as if he simply observed and knew in an external way what was going on in the world. On the contrary, what goes on in the world is a genuine manifestation of the living process which is his own nature; and it also makes a difference to him, for it makes possible the novelty of adaptation, the emergence of new actualities, and the appearance of real possibilities, which otherwise would not be available to him. History, historical occurrences in time, are real to him, for him, and in him.

Now what is involved here is a radical historicizing not only of the order of nature and of all that is in nature, but also of deity in his concrete reality. A Christian may be allowed to say that, if ever there were a philosophy which took seriously the kind of portrayal of God in relation to his world which we find in the biblical record, it is the philosophy of process. But just as in the biblical record God remains God throughout the story, not in spite of but precisely *because of* his capacity for relating himself afresh to every exigence, every human action, every event in the natural order and in the historical sequence; so in process-thought God remains God, forever "creating" new possibilities and forever employing the world's occasions for the fulfilment of his purpose, which we may describe as the specific "subjective aim" which is characteristic of deity. God is faithful, the Bible tells us; the world in process, and the chief principle of explanation in that processive world, are self-consistent and harmonious, the philosophers of process affirm. These two assertions are remarkably similar.

If God is the source of all possibilities, as "primordial deity", there is a sense in which he may be called abstract and "eternal"; but God is also infinitely related to and influenced by the world, and hence as "consequent deity" is concrete and "everlasting". In other words, while the possibilities are "eternal" and while they are "abstract" until in one way or another they are actualized, the actualizations which are selected and used by God for further achievement of his purpose of good in the world are themselves concrete and in process; when taken into God they establish deity as being himself also concrete and processive. But it is the dynamic, processive, and becoming aspect which, in one sense, is more important to us than the abstractive aspect. Thus there is a polarity in this concept of God: he is both abstract and concrete; he is both "eternal" and "everlasting"; he is both himself and yet endlessly related; he is both transcendent and immanent; he is both the chief principle of explanation and yet participant, working with, and influenced by, all that is to be explained. But the priority is with the concrete, not with the abstract, set of terms.

What then of "evil" in the world? Here three things are to be said. First, in a world which is in movement, which is an evolutionary process, and which is at the same time "open-ended", in which novelty is present and new possibilities are always becoming available, there is inevitably the chance of error. Error here means that the adjustment of means to end, the fulfilment of end by means, and the consequent adaptation of each succeeding occasion to the aim which is its basic identity, may be missed in this or that given instance. If the world were conceived as in some fashion a static entity, such error would hardly be possible to understand; but in a world which is processive and dynamic, error is not only possible but on occasion it is highly likely. There is always some element of "risk" in such a process. Furthermore, as the process goes on there is always the possibility that what we might call "backwaters" will remain. Here and there, in this instance and in that, there will be a certain recalcitrance, negativity, a refusal to move for-

ward for the creation of greater good and towards more
widely shareable and more widely shared life. And
since the world has a radical freedom, being in fact the
realm of choice, such as we know at the human level
in conscious decision but which in differing mode is
present at every level, this may be not only a "natural"
recalcitrance but a quite definitely elected refusal to move.

In the second place, it is characteristic of God, in his
"consequent" aspect, to take into himself *all* that has in
fact occurred. Whether this be good or evil, whether it
be directed to further prospective fulfilment or a denial
of that end, whether it be adjustment or maladjustment: all is accepted by God and in one way or another
can be used by him. None the less, he remains *God*,
which means that he is ceaselessly working towards the
most widely shared good. Hence a mysterious but
genuine part of the divine agency in the world (of which
more will be said later in this chapter) is the way in
which the error, the maladjustment, the refusal to move
forward, the "evil" in the world, precisely because (and
precisely in the degree that) it enters into the divine
concern, can become the occasion for new possibilities
of good. In other words, God makes the best of everything, even of that which we can only describe as "evil";
and out of it is able to distil goods, some of which otherwise would not have been in the realm of genuine
possibility.

The third point in respect to "evil" may be ap-
proached by noting that in speaking of the creative
process we have been obliged to use the word "good" to
describe what God is "up to" in the world. The word
has been employed to indicate that which can be shared
for mutual enrichment; and this use leads us to the

description of God as being essentially "Love". It is of the nature of love to pour itself out for others; to take into itself all that is made available to it; to absorb the evil which is there and out of it to distil something good; and to do all this not for self-aggrandizement but for the benefit of the entire relationship in its widest and richest sense. Love is both self-giving and unitive. Thus we may say that God is love because he is infinitely related; he is love because he enters into and participates in his creation; he is love, supremely, because he absorbs error, maladjustment, evil, everything that is ugly and unharmonious, and is able to bring about genuine and novel occasions of goodness by the use of material which seems so unpromising and hopeless. So the third point about evil is that in the concrete world of experience, and especially in human relationships, we see that it may provide the opportunity for deepening love and for widening participation in the good—although this must never be taken to mean that evil is, in itself, a good. It is not; but it may be used *for* good.

The objection has been raised by some that such a view of God as that found in process-thought may be satisfactory enough on the basis of philosophical enquiry, but that it provides no "religiously available" deity for men. This suggests two questions about which something must be said.

First, does this concept of God in fact arise from genuine experience or is it purely theoretical? To this we have already given the answer; the God who is here portrayed is not derived from theoretical considerations alone, although of course these have entered into the picture since God is taken to be "the chief principle of explanation". But the way in which he has been described has come in the main from the observable facts of experience and from our observation of how things go in the world. Hence God as here "described" (an almost blasphemous word!) is God as he has been encountered or seen in his workings in the creative process. But—and this is the second question—is such a God in any sense describable as "personal"? Here we are obliged first of all to define what should be meant by the adjective. Whitehead, for example, seems to have been in two minds about the viability of the idea of God as "personal", largely because he felt that as *commonly* used the term was overtly anthropomorphic and did not provide adequate explanation of that kind of experience which stresses the sheer "given-ness" of process. We must agree that if "personal", when applied to deity, means that God is to be taken as an enlarged replica of what *we* know as person, as if he were (so to say) "a very big man", then it is obvious that the adjective is entirely inappropriate. If, on the other hand, we define more carefully what is meant by "personal", perhaps there can be no objection to employing the word when speaking of deity. By "personal" we can and I believe we should mean such characteristics as awareness and self-awareness, capacity to communicate or enter into active-reactive relationships, freedom of action within the limits of consistency and possibility, etc. All these characteristics are quite readily applicable to deity as seen in process-thought. In that sense, then, God may properly be called "personal"—provided of course, that we are constantly on guard against restricting the sense of these "personal" elements in him to the merely human level on which we ourselves know personality.

So far we have not discussed the area of human life which is known as the "religious experience", the awareness of the "more-than-human" impinging on ordinary experience. Yet this kind of experience is certainly central in the historical and theological development of the concept of God. In the main, it should be noted, process-philosophers have been quite ready to use such religious experience as part of the data which must be taken seriously in the effort to understand the world. They have accepted the fact that vast numbers of members of the human race have spoken or written about some such awareness, however it may have been conceived, of a presence which is believed to be more than human, and they have told us that they have experienced a power that seems to come from beyond, above, and below the level of human enabling. How this sense of presence and power has been expressed in words is another matter, differing from age to age, place to place, and culture to culture. But the awareness of "the sacred" is too widespread to be dismissed by any responsible thinker. The history of religion is the continuing story of the refining of the meaning of such awareness. In primitive man, sheer power may well have been dominant in his conception of the meaning of the sacred. But as men became more and more aware of moral principles and as their thinking was "rationalized", the way in which the sacred was understood, the way in which men came to interpret the more-than-human, was in terms of love and of "persuasion" (as Whitehead put it), although it never lost the awesome quality which evoked from them worship and adoration. There was a gradual substitution of tenderness for sheer power, of goodness for omnipotence, and of deep and intimate concern for arbitrary dictatorship. So the religions of the world, as they have developed through the centuries, have tended to react against despotic conceptions of deity and to regard the sacred as holy love.

As this movement has proceeded, there has also been an increasing readiness to relate the so-called religious experience to the aesthetic experience—to the sense of the harmonious and the beautiful as this was perceived by a deeply felt appreciative capacity in man. And here we come to a matter of quite enormous significance. We have already emphasized that in the refusal to separate primary from secondary qualities process-thought has reversed the over-rationalizing philosophical tendency of western man. Feeling-qualities, the sense of empathetic identification, and the valuational aspect in all human experience have been given serious attention by most process-thinkers; this was why words like "good" and "love" and "harmony", and their opposites, could be used with some freedom in the preceding discussion. What this suggests to us is that religion, as an inescapable element in that human experience, is one of the ways—indeed it may be the chief way—in which man feels his way into, finds identification with, and becomes participant in, the ongoing "movement of things".

If this is so, the experience is not only with the "movement of things" but with the dynamic power which makes that movement actual; in a word, with God himself. There can be no doubt that countless men have felt themselves caught up into what in more thoughtful moments they have regarded as the working of supreme actuality as it operates ceaselessly in the world. They tell us that they have known themselves to be empowered in this relationship. Their limited concern for their own self-hood and for self-assertion has been redeemed, they insist, into concern for others and for greater good. They say that they have been refreshed, invigorated, renewed, made better because of it. And they declare that they have experienced the judgment of an all-inclusive love on their pettiness and pride, while at the same time they have been the recipients of a forgiveness or acceptance which comes when their previous stupidity and cupidity have in some strange fashion been taken away and they have been given the opportunity and occasion for genuine enrichment in fellowship with their human brethren. In other words, they tell us that they have known the energizing of God in their own experience as the loving Companion who is also the sovereign Ruler —not the despot, not the oriental sultan or dictator, but the One who "rules" and who works for good which can be in "widest commonalty spread". They are sure that precisely in his boundless creativity God can guarantee the eventual triumph of good, no matter what may be the evil with which he must work and the risks which such working necessarily implies. Through suffering, they say, we can know joy; and this is because God's patient self-identification with his world enables him to use its anguish, which he knows and shares in himself, for the accomplishment of gloriously good ends.

In our common human experience, God is often "the void", as Whitehead once said, although he said it in a very different context. We are not aware of him, in any vivid sense or perhaps in any sense at all; he is present to us in the very fact of our feeling of his absence. Again, his activity as participant love can make him seem to us our "enemy", which once more is Whitehead's word; God's supreme goodness makes our lives look shoddy

and cheap and we are brought to a self-imposed judgement by the love which is ultimately sovereign over all
things. But there can also come times, as Whitehead
went on to say, when "God the void" and "God the
enemy" becomes "God the companion", the One who
is somehow sensed as "with us"—perhaps dimly and
vaguely sensed, perhaps more vividly and acutely sensed,
but none the less sensed, in this or that moment of our
experience.[1] The basic act of faith, which is open to any
and every man, is to live his whole life on the assumption that such moments, when love is known and life
is shared in a deep relationship of love one with another,
are in very truth the disclosure of the structure of things
and of the dynamic power which moves in and through
the world; and hence that the "actual entity" which
men have called God has both "the nature and the
name" of Love.

In a beautiful passage, which comes after his criticism
of more traditional concepts of God as despotic ruler,
moral governor, or unrelated first cause above and beyond the creation, Whitehead once wrote:

> There is in the Galilean origin of Christianity yet
> another suggestion which does not fit very well with
> any of the three main strands of thought. It does not
> emphasize the ruling Caesar, or the ruthless moralist,
> or the unmoved mover. It dwells upon the tender

[1] A critic may point out, correctly enough, that Whitehead uses
the terms "void", "enemy", and "companion" to describe the
historical development of the concept of God. However I think
that my "existential" use of the terms here is not alien to his
more general line of thought; and in any event I find the words
extremely apt in making the point I am arguing in this paragraph.

elements in the world, which slowly and in quietness operate by love; and it finds purpose in the present immediacy of a kingdom not of this world. Love neither rules nor is unmoved; also it is a little oblivious as to morals. It does not look to the future; for it finds its own reward in the immediate present.[1]

B

For our purposes it has been convenient to follow the traditional sequence in philosophical theology, in which it is customary for a presentation of the nature of God to precede rather than follow the discussion of his manner of operation in creation. This, as I say, has been the usual procedure; and yet in the Christian theological structure God in fact is known for what he is through a study of what he *does*. In theological language, this means that his revelation or self-disclosure, which is made primarily through what are sometimes styled his "mighty acts" in nature and history, has been the clue to his nature. In process-thinking, certainly, the same is true—the meaning of the concept of God is not derived from abstract theory but from observation of the world and its concrete actuality. Let us then proceed at once to a discussion of the Divine Activity as this is generally understood by process-thinkers.

The first point is to repeat what we have already noted, namely that for process-thought God's relationship to his world, and his working within it, are never conceived as an external relationship or as an arbitrarily

---

[1] *Process and Reality*, pp. 520–21.

intrusive action. God is *in* his world; or perhaps it would be better to say that the world is in God. For the most part process-thought has been *panentheistic* in tendency. "Panentheism" was first used by the German writer Krause during the last century. It is to be sharply distinguished from *pantheism*, which would identify God and the world. For the panentheist everything which is not in itself divine is yet believed to be "in" God, in the sense that he is regarded as the circumambient reality operative in and through, while also more than, all that is not himself; or conversely all which is not God has its existence within his operation and nature. Here of course we are using pictorial language; but from this there can be no escape, no matter what philosophical orientation we may adopt.

It is very important to see that panentheism is intended to be a mean between the absentee-God of deism —who is indeed also the God of much popular Christian teaching and preaching and of much supposedly orthodox theology—and the pantheistic God who is simply identified with the world as it is—an identification sometimes without qualification but more frequently with certain reservations that are thought to safeguard moral distinctions. Spinoza's phrase *Deus sive natura* is a succinct statement of pantheism. Panentheism, on the other hand, attempts to preserve the relative independence of the world-order, while at the same time it insists that God cannot be envisaged as totally separated from or alien to that order. Indeed we might say that the adoption of such a panentheistic view is the only way in which *genuine* theism can be maintained, if by theism (as distinguished from pantheism and deism) we mean that God and the world are not thought to be identical even though they are taken to be intimately and necessarily related one to the other. In theism generally, however, God is seen as "cause" and the world as only "effect", in such fashion that without God there could be no world at all. The corollary of that view is that one could say that without the world God theoretically speaking might indeed still be God. But for the process-thinker if God is in fact *creator*, with creative activity in love as his very heart, then he cannot be the *God he is*, and hence not really God, unless there is a world in which his creativity is expressed and which itself is an expression of that creativity, and unless he is "affected" by that world and what happens in it.

Since for process-thought God and the world are thus most intimately related, the world may be described as "organic" to the divine reality. It is not an afterthought of God, who before it was "made" had existed in isolation. (Incidentally the Christian doctrine of the triunity of God does not really demand this, despite frequent assertions to the contrary.) Neither is the world adjectival to God in the sense that what happens in it is expressive of, but without real effect upon, the divine reality. We have already noted this point and we shall be returning to it again later in our discussion.

Furthermore, process-thought does not build on so-called "intrusions" or "interventions" of deity in the created world. Since nothing is "outside" God and since he is the chief explanatory principle in and for all things, although the fact of creaturely freedom demonstrates that he is not the *only* one, it would be absurd to speak of his "intruding" or "intervening" in his world. He is always *there*, or else the world could not and would not be there either. Yet this does not deny the possibility that there may be "fuller" or "deeper" or "richer" instances of the divine operation in this or that particular area or aspect of nature and history. What Gerard Manley Hopkins so beautifully styled "the dearest freshness deep down things" is by no means excluded in process-thought; indeed it is emphasized. Nor is the particularly vivid manifestation of that "freshness" in given times and places ruled out of the picture. On the contrary, it is precisely in such a picture as that which is provided by process-thought, that particularities of this kind are given point and significance in respect to the entire dynamic movement of creation. But they are not seen as *un-related* instances, to be taken simply by themselves; rather they are *indicative* of the total structure and of the dynamic of God's operation. Hence they may be seen as possessing a peculiar importance for our interpretation of its meaning.

We are thus brought back to the notion of "importance", to which reference has been made in our earlier discussion. In that discussion, we spoke of moments which objectively have an unusually striking quality and subjectively evoke an unusually vivid response, providing us with significant clues to the nature of the process in its entirety. As we then said, such moments have their "importance" in that they illuminate what has gone before, are in themselves a kind of concentration of what is actually present, and provide new opportunities and possibilities both for understanding (which is the "subjective" side) and for that emergence of novelty in concrete experience (which guarantees "objectivity") which is the occasion for further creative advance as the process continues on its way. The emergence of living matter, the appearance of consciousness in such living matter, and the coming into existence of moral valuation and appreciative awareness in human life are instances of "importance" which should be obvious to any observer of the world-process.

But since this is true, the creation is best understood as an order in which new levels do in fact make their appearance. They are not to be explained reductively in terms of what has preceded them; on the other hand they are not to be seen as entirely unrelated to all that has gone before. They are indeed genuinely new, they have the quality of emergent novelty, yet they are not in total contradiction to the preceding sequence of events which has prepared for them and made their appearance possible. And once they have occurred, they inaugurate new possibilities on their own level and they open up a range of experience which without them would not be available. Pierre Teilhard de Chardin has made much of this in his widely read *The Phenomenon of Man*, but long before the publication of that volume C. Lloyd-Morgan in his Gifford lectures had indicated the significance of such "emergents", along with the "importance" (although this is not his, but Whitehead's, word) which they possess both in the ongoing movement of the world and as a way of our grasping of the meaning of that world *in its ongoing movement*. In some sense they are the activity of God, just as the whole process is also in some sense that activity.

How then does God "act" in his world? Before discussing this question, in general, following the line of Whitehead's picturing of the matter, there are some prior considerations to which brief reference must be made.

First, process-thought would insist that it is always through the activity of God that things come to pass, although God is not the *only* agent in creation. On the one hand, the divine activity is the ultimate grounding for events; it provides the ultimate efficient cause which turns mere possibility into sheer actuality. On the other hand, God is the final *end* of all that comes to pass, since it is for the fulfilment of his purpose (or, in Whiteheadian language, for the "satisfaction" of God's "subjective aim") that the process goes on, with its consistency and with its new emergents. This should not be taken to mean that God is introduced as a sort of "stopgap" for man's ignorance. He is not understood as the God who functions only in those "mysterious" areas in which we are not able as yet to see the connections of past and present. His all-inclusive functioning is the *basic* ground of each and every occurrence; he is *Alpha* and *Omega*, both the origin—although not necessarily in the ordinary temporal sense—of all things and the goal towards which they move. Thus he is the sufficient *ultimate* explanation of what occurs. He is adequate to explain what happens; and he is increasingly shown to be adequate as the process goes forward. Each new event rests back upon and is an expression of, while it also provides genuine fulfilment for, the originative and final purpose which is divine—in one sense, even the "evil" occasion has this reference, although God is not "responsible" for it.

Second, this adequacy does not depend upon God's being recognized as such. The divine activity in the world is for the most part an *incognito* activity, by which I mean that it is divine activity in and through, by and under, "creaturely" occasions. As we emphasized in the preceding lecture, God does not exist nor does he act only to the degree in which he is explicitly seen by the human mind to exist and to act. He is greater than that. He is not simply a mental concept devised by man for his own purposes, but rather he is inescapable as the *supreme* (I repeat, not the *only*) "cause" in the total process of creation and in every moment within that process. The radical freedom found in the world cannot finally overthrow him; his *love* is supreme over all. In *this* sense, it matters little enough whether he is given any particular proper name, although there are other reasons for calling him "God" and certainly we are right in describing him as "Love".

Third, since God is not the great exception, metaphysically speaking, but is himself "the supreme exemplification"of the principles which actually and concretely operate in the world, a study of how the world goes will be the best way in which we can come to understand the nature of the divine activity itself. As we become aware of new and particular concretions which are grasped (or as Whitehead would say "prehended") by us, we are given an insight into the God who provides the data for these and effectively brings them about. As there are enrichments in the process which contribute to new possibilities and hence to the provision of new actual data for "prehension", we are given some understanding of how God is in himself "enriched", so that he is capable of a variety of novel adjustments to which he is entirely adequate without his becoming "more" God than he is—although his deity can be, and is, more adequately expressed and active, and hence more adequately disclosed, in consequence of them.

When, therefore, we use the phrase "God acts", what we are really saying is that the divine causal efficacy, moving towards the fulfilment of the divine aim, is in varying degrees the dominant element in each successive occasion. Were this not the case, there could be no occasion at all, since (as we have seen) God is precisely that factor which provides both the "control" and the "efficacy" which brings the occasion about. On the other hand his control and efficacy operate not by arbitrary (that is to say, independent and "omnipotent") over-ruling, nor by being the *only* active elements in the occasion; but by the persuasive moulding of new possibilities, by redirecting the pressures of prior actualities, by providing new opportunity for advance, and by offering the "lure" which evokes from each occasion in the ongoing process the movement towards satisfaction of its "subjective aim". This aim, it must be remembered, is the identifying quality of each specific actual event as it goes along its own particular routing within the process as a whole. So God as the "principle of concretion" can operate without for a moment reducing the value of, or in any way negating the role played by, the freedom of the creation.

In this conception of the divine activity we see clearly that radical historicizing of the creative process to which we have already called attention as characteristic of process-thought. Notions such as "satisfaction", "subjective aim", "realization", "actualization", "movement", and even "process" itself, have been introduced into the explanation of the world. This is not because such words are supposed to have some kind of vitalistic tinge which will redeem what we have to say from apparent mechanistic suggestions, but because they are in fact required for any genuine understanding of the world and any sound explanation of how things come to be.

The teleological aspect of the picture drawn in process-thought is indeed very clear. In the real world there is no monotonous repetition, no grinding-out of an already predetermined routine, no re-shuffling of a pack of cards. On the contrary, there is a genuinely epigenetic advance in the order of nature and in the realm of history. The mechanisms are certainly there; but they are mechanisms of the kind that we know as elements in an organism, not those which might be more appropriately ascribed to an engine or a machine. They subserve the "ends" of the whole. So novelty *does* occur; there *are* real supervenient occasions; the world is no rigid corpse but is a living and organic (or societal) process.

Finally, genuine, not Pickwickian, freedom is seen to be a genuine constituent of the process. For God does not dictate. He is no tyrant, nor can he act without regard for the created occasions. He persuades, draws out, elicits, provides data for, and is himself enriched by, the new occasions as they occur. He uses the materials of the world as they have come to exist. He works in and through, with and by, for and on behalf of all those actual entities which at any given moment are present. Through his "tenderness" and by means of his "lure", he moves them towards those self-decisions which can bring about great and greater good. He offers ever more widely shared opportunities for enhancement; and throughout the process he works towards the appearance of a realm in which his own satisfaction of aim in a

Suggested diagrammatic representation of Divine
Activity in the world

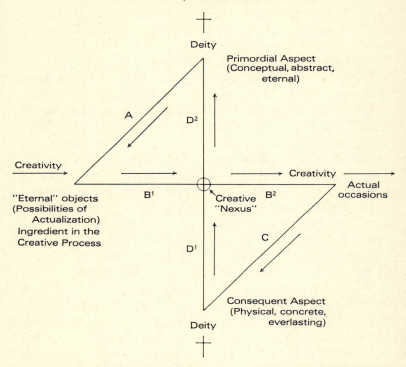

(The author is indebted to two of his former students, the
Reverend Gary McElroy and the Reverend William F. Starr, for
the suggestion that Whitehead's view of Divine Activity might
be represented by some such diagram as is here shown.

(Another possible diagramming will be found in the note
appended to this chapter. For this second diagram the author is
indebted to Professor Donald Sherburne of Vanderbilt University, U.S.A., who has kindly consented to its use. The special
value of Professor Sherburne's diagram is that it avoids the
possible suggestion, in the diagram above, that one is, so to say,
moving *backwards* in following lines A and C, since line B (both
B[1] and B[2]) are intended, in loyalty to process-thought, to repre-
sent the *forward* thrusting of creativity.)

realm of love becomes also the satisfaction of the creaturely aim and hence a sharing in love, as the creation
moves forward towards richer life.

Some explanation is required of the accompanying
diagram, in order to make clearer the way in which the
divine activity is presented in Whitehead's thought—
a presentation which to the writer seems the most
adequate description available to us. It should be
apparent, as we proceed, that this presentation is no
merely speculative scheme but is in fact a description
of that which occurs in the world as we know it. It is an
explanation which, in Plato's phrase, "saves the appear-
ances" by providing a coherent and meaningful account
of what goes on and of why it goes on as it does.

1. In the diagram the vertical line represents deity.
The upper point stands for God in his "primordial"
aspect, abstractly understood as the eternal reality whose
awareness conceptually includes all the possibilities
("eternal objects") denoted by the extreme left point
of the horizontal line; this includes the abstract aspects
or patterns of all that might come to pass in the created
order, envisaged as possibilities for actualization. The
lower point of the vertical line stands for God in his
"consequent" aspect as the recipient of all that has
occurred in the order of creation, hence as concrete and
everlasting in that the factuality of the occasions in the
process have entered into and helped to mould the
divine experience in its capacity for infinite adjustment
and relationship. This aspect of deity is called "physical"
because it is inclusive of the events in "nature" (*physis*)
and is not abstractly conceptual or theoretical.

2. The horizontal line "B¹–B²" represents the process
of the created order. In the first place, the line as a

whole is established on "creativity"; that is, on the potentiality of things to come into existence as concrete actualities. Here we can perhaps find analogies in the "first matter" of Aristotle, the given materiality of Plato, or the initial potency of which Aquinas speaks. In any event, we are concerned to stress the patent fact of a potentiality for event or occurrence as the pre-requisite to our understanding of the world which we know. This horizontal line moves *from* possibilities of actualization, as they are available for the actualization which will produce real entities, *through* the "creative nexus" (of which we shall speak in a moment), *to* the concrete occasions with which we are confronted in their presentational immediacy to us. That is, the horizontal line includes all that actually is going on in the world.

3. The line "A" represents the divine activity through which the possibilities of actualization are brought into concrete and factual existence. Deity, as the principle by which possibilities are actualized, may thus be said to select or "decide for" this or that set of possibilities; hence deity in this aspect may be styled "first" (prior) principle of causation. The line "C" indicates that actual occasions—things as they are brought to be in the world—return to God, or better are received by God. As they are received by him and thus enter into his very life, they bring about that kind of "enrichment" of the divine reality to which we have frequently referred. Once again, it must be made clear that talk of enrichment is not meant to suggest that God becomes any more "God" than he always has been; what is intended by such language is simply that, because God is supremely related to all occasions, these various occurrences provide material for his fuller expression in

relationship with creation and at the same time bring about an enhancement of the divine joy as well as a participation through "suffering" (or sharing as participation) in all that takes place in the world.

4. The line "D^1–D^2" represents the way in which emergence of novelty in the world takes place. The enhancement of the divine life in its consequent aspect has opened up new possibilities of relationship with the creation and has also provided new material through which God may act upon creative potentiality, thus bringing to pass that emergence of novelty which is so genuine an element in our experience and (as our observation informs us) of the world at large. A simple illustration for this might be the historical development of a given human culture. This development, in combination with the natural setting of that culture which provides its *locus*, moves forward to a point at which, out of the rich congeries of events and responses to events made by those who are involved, a new type of response becomes available. The prophet, for example, makes his appearance. He is not *just* the same as the dervish who preceded him; he is not *simply* a "wise man" or sage; he is not *only* the precipitate of a particular historical milieu with its context in the order of nature. He is indeed all of these, but he is something more too. In him there is the appearance of a novel response to a complex situation; and as such, he brings about new ways of understanding and new kinds of adjustment to the world which then may be shared and developed by those who hear him and accept his message.

5. The point of emergence is called the "creative nexus". While there is preparation for it (D^1), there are

also consequences of it, but these are not only along the line of creative advance (B^2) to which we have just referred. There are also new and enhancing opportunities (line D^2) provided for deity, which he employs in his continuous activity of bringing possibility (left point of the horizontal line) into actuality (along line A). This emergence thus will permit enhancement along the line of creativity (B^1), towards the actualizing of still newer occasions of novelty or freshness.

6. Finally we must remember that all this is an ongoing process. Our diagram is at best a kind of "cross-section" of the dynamic movement which is the given reality of the world and of the Divine Activity in the world. So far as we know, there is no "ending" of the movement. It is everlasting in the sense of a continuous and unceasing development, on the whole moving towards fuller realization of heterogenous yet organically inter-related goods, even though there is "evil" with maladjustments, "backwaters", and elected failure to advance at many points along the line.

The Christian thinker may wish to add to, or to modify, this diagram in the light of his distinctive faith. But what is at once apparent, I believe, is that the diagram portrays an onward movement towards continually greater realization of the purpose or "subjective aim" of Deity. And this realization is, at the same time, the increasing satisfaction of the various "subjective aims" or purposes that are the binding-identity of the several actual entities which are "less" than, and have been brought into existence through, the patient, loving and overcoming work of the divine activity. God "expresses" himself in his ceaseless relationship with and participation in the world, whose future in many respects

is "open". The limits set are those given by the divine
intention for fulfilment or "satisfaction", by the possibilities which at any given moment are available for
use in this way, by the "decision" of each actual entity,
and by the finitude of creativity itself which will permit
only specific creaturely occasions to emerge. Each creaturely occasion, however, is always open to further divine
activity in, upon, and through it. And the divine activity
is always present and at work in each occasion. Hence
each occasion (and more particularly every "good"
occasion) may be seen as an "incarnation" of deity under
the conditions of finite creativity.

Appended Note to Chapter II

Another diagram, in this case suggested (as has been
said earlier) by Professor Sherburne, to illustrate the
fashion of the divine activity in the world, would be as
follows.

There are three useful points about this diagram. In
the first place, it indicates the way in which what Whitehead has called "the weaving of God's physical feelings
upon his primordial concepts" constitutes the *consequent* nature of God—that is, how what God "accepts"
into himself as "affects" modify the future on-going
occasions through a modification of God's own use of
the possibilities offered him (X in the diagram). Second,
in *thus* modifying occasions, it will be seen, subjective
aims are provided for the *further* generation of occasions (Y in the diagram). Third, the new possibilities
(relevant to the past, of course) are seen and felt by
God and become the "lure" (in Whitehead's own word)
to which occasions may respond, to their (and to God's)
enrichment.

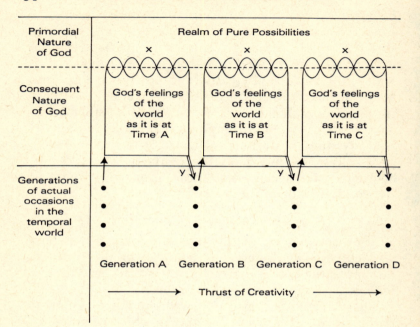

Chapter III

MAN, THE FAMILY, SOCIETY, AND THE MAN OF NAZARETH

A

What is man?

This is a question which has engaged the interest and attention of thinkers in all ages; and the answers which have been given to the question have been many and various. Few representatives of process-thought have devoted themselves to an extended consideration of the question, although almost all of them have made sufficiently clear the approach which they would take to answering it. One of the most explicit discussions of the matter is by Professor Hartshorne, who in a short but stimulating essay entitled "The Unity of Man and The Unity of Nature"[1] has dealt with some aspects of the meaning of human nature in relation to the cosmic setting for human life. Scattered references may be found in the writings of Professor Whitehead and these have been collected in a small volume called *Alfred North Whitehead: His Reflections on Nature and Man.*[2] Of course Père Teilhard had a full-length treatment in *The Phenomenon of Man* and an off-tangent discussion in *The Future of Man* as well as in *The Divine Milieu*, where his main interest however was in making sense of

[1] Included in *The Logic of Perfection* (Open Court Press, La Salle, Ind., 1962).

[2] Edited by Ruth Nanda Anshen (Harper & Row, New York, 1961).

man's religious experience and showing its abiding
significance in a world which is in process. Much of
what Teilhard says is of great importance. However, his
primary concern is to portray man's development and
forecast man's future in the light of evolutionary
development yet also and specifically in the context of
the Christian faith. In this lecture, which like the
others in this series is intended as a general exposition
of process views rather than a Christian development
of them, we shall not make as full use of his teaching as
we shall of that in other representatives of the school.

We start our exposition by reiterating that process-
thought inevitably regards man not as a "thing" but as a
living movement or process. That is to say, human
nature is not taken as a static entity, a fixed substance,
about which predications may be made with equal
fixity. Man is a dynamic being; indeed it is more correct
to say that he is "becoming man" than that he "is" man.
Hence, if we wish to understand the meaning of manhood we must look to the movement from potentiality
to actuality; we must seek to understand something of
what psychologists would call "the dynamics of personality". The poet says that "man never is/but wholly
hopes to be". The attitude which these words suggest
is central in what process-thinkers say about human
nature.

In consequence, therefore, man must first of all be
seen as a finite process of becoming, with recognition of
his dependence upon environmental factors both natural
and historical. Certainly no man is isolated from nor
independent of his environment; neither is he independent of the long series of past occurrences which have
entered into the circumstances of his emergence as a

thinking being who possesses a certain quality of aesthetic responsiveness and a certain capacity for valuation. Man is more than an animal who can think. He is indeed the end-product of a long evolutionary development; yet his appearance as a genuine emergent has introduced novelties which are characteristic of human rather than animal existence. We shall speak of these in a moment.

Not only is man dependent upon his past and upon his present environment; he is also in himself a "projective movement"—he looks to and moves towards the future. In other words, the very fact that he is in process implies that he has a drive towards fulfilment. He is made *for* something. One might put it in this fashion: the meaning of human nature is to be found in its ceaseless striving towards fulfilment in manhood. This is man's subjective aim, to use again the Whiteheadian phrase. Man looks to, moves towards, and is identified by the fulfilment which will establish him as actually being what already he is becoming. Of course this must not be regarded as an always consciously present and vividly realized factor in his experience; most of the time, doubtless, any given man is not *thinking* about these things at all. But he is *living with* this reference implicit in all that he does, says, and thinks. This is his *project*, so to say. Interestingly enough, the Sartrian notion of man's *pour-soi* or projective self, as distinguished from his sheer given-ness as *en-soi*, has a considerable similarity to the general process-idea which we are expounding, whatever may be the differences between the two in statement and interpretation.

Teilhard has spoken of man's appearance from the realm of biological existence, which he calls the *bio-*

sphere, as the appearance of the *noo-sphere*, the realm of thought. There can be no question that a specific, although not the only specific, quality of man as emergent is his ability to engage in conscious thought. Hence we may say that man is an unusually strange and complex being; his physiological existence is "complicated" by the presence of intellection, the activity in him which we call "mind". He can and he does *think*. But the description of man as a rational or intellectual animal, familiar in the Middle Ages, is dangerous unless full recognition is also given to the feeling-tones which are as much a part of human existence as is human rationality. Here once again there is a remarkable similarity between certain emphases in Whitehead as well as in other process-thinkers and the strong insistence of contemporary existentialism on the centrality of the "subjective" feelings and of self-awareness in human experience.

There is a further fact which requires attention. Man is a *valuing* creature. He is able to concern himself with goodness, truth and beauty—to use the familiar platonic triad. He finds himself making judgements of good and bad, right and wrong; he speaks of truth and error; he is aware of harmony or beauty and disharmony or ugliness. Furthermore he is able to set before him "ideals", which he then seeks to achieve; and to envisage purposes which he accounts as good for him and also good in themselves, which he then feels called to pursue. He is able to appreciate; indeed it has been suggested that man might be described not so much as the rational animal as the appreciating animal. Doubtless all this has its basis in his instinctual life; nonetheless, the devotion which a man can develop towards that which he "likes" and

which he finds "worthy" is at a different level and in a
higher degree of intensity—it is qualitatively of a different order—than the apparently similar capacity of, say,
a dog to react favourable or unfavourably to the various
stimuli which are presented to it.

For process-thought, then, man is an organism with
an aim. His physical, biological, psychological, and
rational life, as well as the emotional and aesthetic aspects so basic to his existence, are more or less in process
of integration into a *unity of direction*; and the "will"
of man is directed towards the fulfilment of this aim in
a fashion which he judges to be good. It is indeed possible for man to sink into sheer quasi-mechanical or
quasi-biological responses; but deep in himself, and
sometimes despite himself, he has the feeling that to
sink to a level which is less than *total* organic response
(including intellect and valuation) is nothing short of a
denial of his manhood. It is hardly necessary to repeat
that none of this need be vividly felt nor clearly recognized as present. Man's purposive existence may express
itself in all sorts of hidden ways and under many odd
names. But it is there, none the less, as integral to his
selfhood and as that which constitutes him distinctively
as man.

Acting in and through nature, dependent on nature,
existing as an historical being moving in process towards
fulfilment, compounded of "body" and "mind", capable
of appreciation, valuation, and feeling, man is also
supremely a social creature. He is on the way to becoming human insofar as he is in deep communion with
his fellows. The kind of individualism which would
think of each man as being in and of himself a discrete
entity is from the beginning ruled out by process-

thought as an absurd impossibility. For in this philosophy, as we have seen, societal considerations are so important that any picture of man must not only include them but must include them in a very high degree of intensity. This is why family and friends, tribe and nation, and many other kinds of grouping are natural to man; indeed, they are essential in making him what he is and they are so much part of him that no man can be understood, or can understand himself, in isolation from these various groups to which by necessity he belongs.

This does not mean, however, that man is simply like an ant in an anthill. He is not *lost* in the mass of humanity, in which he would be so utterly submerged that he would also be in danger of losing whatever it is that gives him personal identity. On the contrary, it is precisely through his belonging with his fellows that he *finds* his identity. To be a person means not to be an individual in any isolationist or solitary sense, but to be open to, influenced by, and influencing, other men who are also persons. Each man has his own subjective aim; each man has his own fulfilment. But these are discovered by him in the company of others, with whom relationship is sustained on a more than merely external level. "Deepest commonalty", a phrase we have used earlier, is characteristic of human nature as we know and as we experience it in ourselves and as we observe it in the history of the human race.

Something must now be said of man in his sexuality, although so far as I know this has not been a matter of particular discussion by process-thinkers. Yet its importance in the process-view of man should be clear. The reality of human sexuality is a patent fact; and it would seem to be intimately tied in with man's total organic movement, which as we have seen includes his physiology, biology, and psychology, as well as his appreciative (and hence his aesthetic), valuational, and feeling qualities. It is also associated with man's drive towards the fulfilment which is available to him only in community or society.

Man certainly is a sexual being; but so also are apes. And so, for that matter, are "organisms" at lower levels of nature! But in man, sexuality is of a different sort from that of the ape. In man it is not simply the drive towards reproduction nor is it merely the satisfaction of physical needs or desires. It includes these, but in man as an emergent of the kind we have outlined, sexual instinct has as its context the thrust towards fulfilment in relationship with another of his own human kind. The feeling-tones and the physical acts associated with human sexuality are characterized by the possibility of self-giving and mutuality, reaching finally to the establishment of faithful union of one person with another. In that union two lives are brought together in the deepest way, the physical relationship serving as the expression of a fully personal union involving and including the total life of each partner. This qualitative aspect of sexuality in man makes it different from sexuality in the animal world. And with it goes the place of the family in man's existence. The family is the smallest group or society to which man belongs; but as anthropologists have lately been insisting, it is a society that is an enriching as well as an abiding factor in the history of the race from primitive times to the present day, however various may be the forms which in different cultures it has assumed.

Whitehead and others have written admirably of man in his societal development when it reaches the level of "civilization". So soon as the human race reaches the level of shared appreciation, ordered and agreed convictions as to ends or aims to be sought after and if possible achieved, and a pattern of common life in which the mutuality and sharing known at the personal level can be broadened in more or less formal communal patterns, we can speak of the appearance of civilization. The very word—having to do with a "city" and hence indicative of social relationships of a high order of intensity—shows that we have here a reflection of man's integral belonging-with-others. Whatever may be the level of a given society, it can and does develop such sharing, such participation in agreed values, such mutuality in pursuit of them; and it leads to the appearance of a "culture" which expresses such agreements and aims at their implementation.

All this is clear enough when we consider the long story of man on this planet. As Teilhard has insisted, one of the important developments of the last few centuries of human history has been the growth of a world-view of civilization. Indeed such a view has become essential. The unity of the race, accomplished to a large degree through economic pressures, increased travel, mutual interdependence, and the like, has more and more become a possibility; and it has now been recognized as a *necessity* if wars are to be avoided, general peace ensured, and true human development allowed. Teilhard relates this movement towards the planetary unity of civilizations with what he describes as the increasing convergence of men in a consciousness which is super-individual and with the passing years more and more super-national; and he has some specifically Christian things to say about that movement and its meaning. But of the fact itself there can be little doubt, whatever may be our religious reading of its significance. The quality of such a world-civilization, along with that which is characteristic of smaller expressions of civilized human life, has been beautifully and movingly described in the last sections of Whitehead's *Adventures of Ideas*.

One point, so far hardly mentioned in this discussion of man, needs to be introduced here. At any stage of development, man as a person in community and also the community of persons who are moving towards "civilization", may be deflected from following the main "aim", and hence may become either a backwater in the ongoing movement or be victims of maladjustment so serious that damage is done not only to the whole dynamic process but also to the smaller organisms or societies, including man himself as such an organic entity. The results can be tragic and terrible. Anti-social choices and anti-social patterns of behaviour, by which we mean choices and patterns harmful to man in community and to each man in his own integration, have occurred and do occur. Through these choices and by acceptances of these patterns each man can harm himself as well as others. That is, he can (and observably he often does) elect to live in self-contained ways, denying his drive towards fulfilment in manhood, failing to share in rich commonalty with his fellows, seeking satisfactions which are so partial, limited, and defective that they impede and damage his basic drive as a total personal organism—an organism which is on the way to realization of its richest and widest possibilities.

This is what the higher religions of man have called

"sin"; it may be given some other name by so-called "secular" thinkers, but the fact itself is plainly to be seen and the tragedy of it is very clear. Process-thought has taken account of this in its own way. We have seen in an earlier lecture that the presence of "evil" is not for a moment denied in such thought; neither is there any minimizing of the reality of its effect in hindering the on-going of creative occasions, with the dreadful results that inevitably follow. It is also said by process-thinkers, however, that there are ways in which evil can be and is being absorbed by the Divine Activity and hence made eventually to serve good. This does not mean that there is no real loss; and it may be that *some* evil is not as such "redeemable". But a Christian reading of process-philosophy could very well make its own the words of the Psalmist, "God maketh even the wrath of man"—and the maladjustment and failure in nature too, we might add—"to turn to his praise"—which is to say, to be mysteriously transmuted into opportunities and occasions for the realization of possible goods.

The various emphases to which we have alluded in this lecture have illustrated once again, I hope, the way in which process-thought finds the created order a unity of an organic kind and insists that God himself is the supreme exemplification of the principles needed to understand and explain that creation. For man here is both a microcosm of the universe and at the same time and in certain significant respects an anticipation of what Teilhard called the *Omega-point* or God. Mutual dependence and interdependence, deepening inter-relationship all along the line of advance, community or sociality, participation in a common life, the presence of a drive towards satisfaction of the subjective aim, and above all the directive or projective aspect which is so closely related to that aim: here we have "in little" what in the universe at large we find in other ways. Here too we have the reflection in manhood and in human society of the nature of Deity and the divine agency in the world.

We shall now turn to see how at least *some* process-thinkers are prepared to relate all this to the strange and compelling, yet unquestionably human, figure of Jesus of Nazareth. He is One with whom many of them feel obliged to come to terms, for (as Emerson once said) his name is "not so much written as ploughed" into the history and experience of the human race.

B

Many process-philosophers, a general summary of whose views we have been presenting in these lectures, are not directly interested in theological matters; many of them who are sympathetic to the insights of Christian faith would not wish to adopt for themselves the designation of "believing Christian". Why then should *some* of them write as they do about Jesus Christ? One would hardly expect a discussion either of the life or of the significance of Jesus of Nazareth in such philosophically oriented studies of nature and history, or even in what little about human nature they have written. It is all the more interesting, therefore, that we do in fact find in certain of these thinkers frequent reference to the Man of Nazareth and in one or two instances evaluations of his significance which one might expect more from theologians than from philosophers.

I believe that part of the answer to my question—
why some process-thinkers have written as they have
about Jesus—is to be found in some remarks from Whitehead which I shall quote later in this lecture. In the
picture of Jesus presented to us in the gospels and
treasured in the Christian "memory" (to use a word of
Professor John Knox), they see a "revelation in act" of
that which a sound philosophical understanding of the
world can discern "in theory". But perhaps there is also
something else. I have heard Professor Hartshorne say
that one must take with the utmost seriousness two
biblical texts: "God is love" (1 John 4:16) and the
"Great Commandment" ("Thou shalt love the Lord thy
God with all thy heart, and with all thy soul, and with
all thy mind" [Matthew 22:37 and parallels]). The
One who *said* the latter and who in his life *embodied*
a human expression of the former is on any reckoning
an "important" person. So a thoughtful man is led to
ask who he is and what his life can mean.

Of course in *one* process-thinker we should be sur-
prised if there were not such a theological interest—
Teilhard de Chardin, who was both a Christian and a
Jesuit priest. In his writings there is explicit acceptance
of the traditional Catholic doctrine about Jesus and yet
also a development of that doctrine with special
emphasis on the cosmic Christ adumbrated in the
Pauline literature and expounded by Teilhard in the
evolutionary perspective. We shall rely, however, on
three representative English process-thinkers—C. Lloyd-
Morgan, Hartshorne, and Whitehead—who are not
theologians and whose interest is not directed specifically
towards elucidating Christian ideas. The variety of their
thought about Jesus will be apparent but so also will be

their agreement that the person and action of Jesus is of importance in any thorough-going metaphysical system and above all in such a scheme as evolutionary or process views of the world demand. Our procedure will be by the use of quotations from each writer, followed by comment. I believe the quotations, in each case fairly brief, are indicative of the general position of the writers.

First, then, and very briefly, some words from Lloyd-Morgan. In concluding his Gifford Lectures[1] Lloyd-Morgan explicitly avows his own Christian faith and asserts that ". . . the Divine Personality shines through the Unique Individuality of the Christ". This statement he interprets in the light of his conviction that "to be emergent in some human persons falls within the Divine Purpose". The *Nisus* working through the whole course of events has in Jesus revealed himself in a specially vivid manner. This is perhaps the most definite statement from any process-thinker of the significance of Jesus. Yet Lloyd-Morgan is not alone in his estimate of the importance of Jesus for the philosopher who would take account of *all* the facts in nature, history, and human experience.

Professor Hartshorne, who has much more to say on this matter, believes that "the Christian idea of a suffering deity" "symbolized by the Cross, together with the doctrine of the Incarnation"[2] may legitimately be taken as a symbolic indication of the "saving" quality in the process of things which despite the evil that appears yet

[1] C. Lloyd-Morgan: *Life, Mind, Spirit* (Williams & Norgate, London, 1911).
[2] C. Hartshorne: *Philosophers Speak of God*, p. 15 (University of Chicago Press, 1953).

makes genuine advance a possibility. He tells us in *Reality as Social Process*[1] that he is sure that "the doctrine of the Incarnation enshrined important religious truth"; on the other hand he is very doubtful whether the traditional dogma of "two natures in one person" can withstand criticism. None the less, he is prepared to allow the legitimacy of the language which speaks of Jesus as "in some sense" divine, provided we "remember that in some sense or degree every man" may also be said to be divine. He has other objections of this same sort to traditional theological interpretations—objections with which one must have a large measure of agreement. I have myself discussed these at some length in a book[2] on the person of Christ; a consideration of them would not be relevant in our present context.

Yet for Professor Hartshorne, and I give here an extended quotation,

> "Jesus was a man who suffered, mentally and physically, in intense degree, and not alone upon the cross. Thus his acceptance of suffering symbolizes the supreme value of humanity. The first of men dies the death of a slave. But should we not go further. Jesus was termed the Christ, the self-manifestation of God."

Hartshorne remarks that while "many theological and philosophical doctrines" of the traditional kind have asserted that "being divine means precisely, and above all, being wholly immune to suffering in any and every sense", yet in his judgement the insight of faith in Jesus as the Christ would rather point logically to the truth

---

[1] C. Hartshorne: *Reality as Social Process*, pp. 150–53 (Collier-Macmillan, New York, 1963).

[2] W. Norman Pittenger: *The Word Incarnate* (James Nisbet & Co. Ltd., and Harper & Row, New York, 1959).

that "there must be suffering in God". Jesus himself
"nowhere asserts or, so far as I can see, even suggests that
God is immune to feeling, suffering, or passivity".
Hence if Jesus is to be taken seriously as a disclosure in
symbol of the divine, God as Jesus reveals him as one
who shares in human anguish even though this is not
the last word.[1]

Again, in *Reality and Social Process*, Hartshorne says
that while he himself has no special christological
formulation to offer the reader, he would make

> "the simple suggestion that Jesus appears to be the
> supreme symbol furnished to us by history of the
> notion of a God genuinely and literally sympathetic
> (incomparably more literally than any man ever is),
> receiving into his own experience the suffering as
> well as the joys of the world."[2]

He affirms his own conviction that "Jesus was, and can
still be, a living and unique symbol";[3] and he argues that
the doctrines about him "name a mystery which is felt
rather than thought; and people may very well feel
differently about different ways of phrasing the
mystery". There can be no doubt of the importance
which Hartshorne finds in the life of Jesus nor of the
Christian intention in his writings.

We have left to the last a remarkable paragraph from
Whitehead, found in *Adventure of Ideas*.[4] Whitehead's
views we have found very useful in these lectures.

[1] All these citations are from the essay "A Philosopher's Assessment of Christianity" in *Religion and Culture*, p. 175 (S.C.M.
Press, London, 1959 and Harper & Row, New York).
[2] Page 24.
[3] Page 152.
[4] A. N. Whitehead: *Adventures of Ideas* (Cambridge University
Press, 1933).

Whether at the end of his life Whitehead would have thought of himself as a Christian is a debatable matter. Some have considered that his comments in the reported dialogues with Lucien Price clearly show that he was not then a Christian. However this may be, his many references to Jesus seem to me of singular interest; and as a matter of fact I believe that Whitehead was and remained a Christian, although not an "orthodox" one.

In the chapter in *Adventures* from which I shall quote, Whitehead is speaking of the contribution of early Christian thought to the developing understanding of the nature of the world's relationship to God. He will go on, in later pages, to make a case for the importance of this contribution for our own time and even to align himself, although with some reservations, with the need for what he calls a "new reformation". I do not know whether this phrase—so often heard to-day and used by him in 1933—had here its first appearance in modern writing. However, this "new reformation", he believes, will incorporate the early Christian insights but will provide for them a new philosophical context in the light of science, philosophy, and other modern ways of seeing the creation and the relationship of God to that creation. Then come these important words:

"The essence of Christianity is the appeal to the life of Christ as a revelation of the nature of God and of his agency in the world. The record is fragmentary, inconsistent and uncertain. . . . But there can be no doubt as to what elements in the record have evoked a response from all that is best in human nature. The Mother, the Child, and the bare manger: the lowly man, homeless and self-forgetful, with his message of peace, love and sympathy: the suffering, the agony, the tender words as life ebbed, the final despair: and the whole with the authority of supreme victory."[1]

I shall not comment on the great insight found in these beautiful words, save to remark that they seem to me to sum up most of what a Christian would wish to say about Jesus. But the point of the quotation, for our present purpose, is found in the first sentence. The "essence of Christianity" is seen by Whitehead as being "the appeal to the life of Christ as revelation of the nature of God and of his agency in the world". There can be little question that Whitehead himself accepted this; he believed that the tenderness, sympathy, and love which were shown in Jesus' life and death are in fact the disclosure of the nature of the Divine Reality who is the chief—although not the only—principle of explanation for all that has been, is, and will be. Furthermore, he believed that the "agency" of God in the world—or what in an earlier lecture we have called "the Divine Activity"—is also of the kind disclosed in the life to which the New Testament bears witness. God in his working, and in his ways of working, is persuasive not coercive power; he is that creative, dynamic, energizing love which was seen by men in the person of Jesus Christ and in Jesus Christ's own working and ways of working. In fact, on the very same page, Whitehead goes so far as to assert that Jesus was the "revelation in act" (that is, in concrete historical occurrence) of what others, and here he cites Plato, have discerned "in theory". This acceptance of what he takes to be "the essence of Christianity" explains why it is

[1] Op. cit, page 214.

possible for Whitehead, in other books such as *Religion in the Making* and in the chapter on science and religion in *Science and the Modern World*, to reveal himself as generally sympathetic to the Christian enterprise. At the same time he has his own very serious reservations and questions, some of which are frankly stated in these particular books, as they are elsewhere in *Adventures of Ideas* and in some of the "table-talk" recorded by Lucien Price in the dialogues.

One of these difficulties comes from his conviction that there is a very sharp contradiction between the despotic deity who as he thinks is dominant in the Old Testament literature and the picture of a loving God taught and revealed by Jesus. It is not, I think, that Whitehead is a modern Marcionite, who would have two "gods": one the creator god of the Old Testament, the other the loving redeemer god of the New. On the contrary, as it seems to me, Whitehead's intention is to say that in much of the Old Testament the nature of the Creator was seriously misunderstood; he was thought of after the model of an oriental sultan because the writers in many instances failed to develop whatever insights they possessed into his nature as creative love. We may wish to disagree with this criticism but we must concede that the "first lessons" in Mattins and Evensong which Whitehead had heard read at church-services in his youth could certainly have given him the impression which he seems to be reporting here.

Another difficulty for Whitehead follows from his uncomfortable feeling, more often hinted than actually expressed, that in traditional Christian theology Jesus has usually been seen as the great anomaly. He is assumed to be the exception to everything else men have learned about God's nature and his "agency". Despite verbal insistence on his humanity, he tends to be portrayed as one who is un-related to the human race save as being intrusive into our midst. As a special case in the sense of being totally unique, he is thought of as the entirely extra-ordinary "act of God" rather than as the exemplary instance of self-disclosure by God. As we noted in an earlier lecture, for Whitehead God himself is not an exception to basic metaphysical principles but rather is their supreme exemplification. So too, it seems to me, he regarded Jesus as being the supreme exemplification, but definitely in terms of genuine human life and experience, of the way God always is and always works. For a Whiteheadian and indeed for any process-thinker, any claim for the uniqueness of Jesus and any notion of his "finality" would require careful re-statement if they are to be accepted; they would need to be brought into congruity with the general line of thought appropriate to such a view of the world as the evolutionary and societal interpretation would provide.

But to return to Whitehead's explicit position, we should observe that he believed that the great virtue of Christianity has been that it is not so much a metaphysic seeking some historical grounding as it is an historical fact and focus (found in Jesus) seeking for metaphysical explanation. The point here, in his own words, is that "Christ gave his life: it is for Christians to discern the doctrine".[1] On the other hand, the metaphysic which Whitehead—and with him other philosophers of process—believe to be valid is indeed a

[1] A. N. Whitehead: *Religion in the Making*, p. 56 (Cambridge University Press, 1926).

metaphysic which is congruous with what is thus disclosed in Jesus.

We have, then, a sort of two-way movement. We can proceed from what men have found in the impact of Jesus. They have been led, often unwillingly, to affirm that Love in its infinite capacity for relationships and its profound participation in that in which it is at work, is the very nature of God himself; they have found in that love the clue to God's way of working in the world. Or on the other hand, we can proceed from what we know about the world itself, about human history, and about human experience. Here the thinker is led to the conclusion that the only adequate explanatory principle of the creation is an energy which is patient, tender, participant, ceaselessly at work in the world, enhanced by that world's happenings as they provide new ranges of possible ways of adjustment, and moving always towards greater good in every nook and cranny.

It is in this context that at least some process-thinkers are prepared to set Jesus of Nazareth. For the Christian, and *a fortiori* for the Christian understanding of the meaning of Jesus' person and work, it may well be that they have made a significant contribution to which we should give the most serious attention.

Chapter IV

THE QUESTION OF DESTINY AND SOME CONCLUDING COMMENTS

A

In this concluding lecture we begin with a discussion of the views of two process-thinkers, Whithead and Hartshorne, in respect to the destiny of man and what is usually called "immortality". In what way does man and his personality have for these thinkers a permanent place both in the on-going process of creation and in the Divine Activity which under-girds and works through that process? Is it possible to speak in their language of an assurance of "life beyond death"? More generally we shall consider whether a process-thinker can make room for some sort of immortality for men. Or in a better way of putting the question, "Does eternal life have any meaning in terms of process-thought?"

On this subject, there is in fact a great variety of opinion among thinkers whose writing can be placed in the category of process-thought. For example, there is Père Teilhard, who spoke as a convinced Roman Catholic although he was also a distinguished representative of the sort of evolutionary thought we have been expounding. It has been said that Teilhard could not accept in any genuine sense the position of his communion on these matters. I do not believe this to be accurate. Both in *The Phenomenon of Man* and in

The Divine Milieu, Teilhard indicated his conviction that the "end" for which man is intended—and not only man in the racial sense but each man specifically—was a relationship with God, conceived as the *Omega-point* or the goal and end of the creative process as well as the transcendent origin and initiator of that process. This relationship, he claimed, would establish for personality an existence through and beyond the termination of the particular finite existence it now enjoys. He envisaged this destiny for persons as accomplished through union with, but not (as some seem to think he meant) absorption in, "the Christ who is to be". The cosmic Christ will "include" within himself all things and all persons who thus become his "body", but they will not be "lost" in him; in "the end" they are to be the truly personal means through whom he expresses himself as the fulfilment of all in all.

Again, Lloyd-Morgan, who was also an avowed Christian, in the last chapters of his Gifford Lectures affirmed that the individuality which emerges at the human level is not an ephemeral phenomenon in the cosmos. On the contrary; for through the ongoing *Nisus* of the creation, which for him is the work of the Eternal Word or (in our language) the Divine Activity, there is a realization of the full potentiality of each individual. Lloyd-Morgan did not discuss the problem at length but it may be said that his view certainly leaves the door open for some conception of immortality. How the conception would be spelled out we do not discover.

We turn now to Professor Whitehead. We find a fairly full statement of his views in the Ingersoll lecture on Immortality, which has been included in the volume

Essays in Science and Philosophy.[1] This lecture we shall summarize in a few minutes. But we should note that Professor Charles Hartshorne, the outstanding contemporary exponent of Whiteheadian thought, is himself not prepared to concede that Whitehead's position, nor his own development of that position, lead necessarily to the belief in a personal immortality. Hartshorne cannot be said to *rule out* this belief, but he feels that there are serious problems in it; we shall also speak of these later. His considered treatment of the question of destiny and immortality may be found in his contribution to the Tillich *festschrift*[2] and in a chapter entitled "Time, Death, and Everlasting Life" in *The Logic of Perfection*.

Whitehead's approach to the question is made through an analysis of the two "realms" of "activity" and of "value". We have seen in a previous lecture that process-thought is not content with the kind of dichotomy between fact and interpretation which has long been popular in some rationalist circles. Whitehead is clear on the point. He insists on the importance of the "feeling-tones", the aesthetic element in all experience, and the reality of human experiences of value. For him these are a genuine part of total experience, quite as real and quite as significant as the experience of the so-called primary qualities. Furthermore, he is highly critical of the sort of philosophical procedure which would abstract these interpretative elements from our confrontation with given fact. In the sheer given-ness of

[1] A. N. Whitehead: *Essays in Science and Philosophy* (Rider & Co, London, 1948).

[2] "A Philosopher's Assessment of Christianity" in *Religion and Culture*: Essays in Honour of Paul Tillich, Ed. W. Leibrecht (S.C.M. Press, London, 1959; Harper & Row, New York).

presentational immediacy coupled with causal efficacy—in things as we actually experience them—both fact and meaning are given together. Or as he puts it, there is no such thing as entirely uninterpreted fact, any more than there is any such thing as an "action" in the world which has no valuation judgement attached to it in the complex reality of human experience.

Since this is true, it is also apparent that when the occasions which appear or occur in the world-process make their contribution to the divine experience, by being received into the consequent aspect of deity, they are received as much more than mere abstractions or bare data without valuational warmth. In the actual and concrete event of their occurring, they have carried with them in their organic richness the worth that they have been thought or found to possess: that is intrinsic to their very occurrence. They have been "valued" because in some sense they were "valuable". They have served a purpose which included an aesthetic element. Further, they have known some genuine satisfaction of their subjective aim. When therefore they are taken into the consequent aspect of deity, to be used in the furthering of God's purpose in creation, they are not *bare* "things", but full and rich and "valuable" occasions—and routing of occasions—in one degree or another. It is true that the world is characterized by what Whitehead called "the perishing of occasions"; that is, the specific concrete events of which the world is made up do not abide as such. They have played their part in the process and have been employed to provide the opportunity for further advance; they no longer can be said to "exist", once this task is accomplished. Yet there *is* something that does abide. This is the *worth*

of such occasions; and it must be remembered that that
worth is itself not abstract or "ideal". Value is not, so to
say, naked or unclothed—for all value requires factuality
for its existence, just as all factuality is possessed of value.

Thus Whitehead can speak of what has been called
by Hartshorne the "divine memory". There is of course
"objective immortality" in the sense that the several
occasions, as they have come into being, realized their
aim, and then "perished" as the process moves on, have
made their specific contribution to the enrichment of
the whole process and have been used by the Divine
Activity in establishing fuller good in wider participation. Beyond this, in the life of God himself—that is,
in his consequent aspect which is always in deepest
inter-relationship with the world in its becoming—these
several occasions or events, with all their worth or value
—and also with recognition of whatever "unworth" or
dis-value may have marked them—are not altogether
lost. They are "remembered", and this in the most
serious sense. For *God* to "remember" does not mean
anything like a simple recollection of that which is now
past and done with. On the contrary, it means that those
events and occasions have so much entered into and so
much become part of Deity in his consequent aspect—
providing new possibilities for relationship, new opportunities for creative advance, new chances for the bringing into actuality of genuine and richer good—that they
are in some deep and real sense integral to the divine
life itself.

The further question, of whether this kind of
"memory" which preserves the reality of such valued
data in the divine life, also carries with it what we might
describe as *subjective* immortality, is not discussed in

Whitehead's essay. It is true that in *Religion in the Making* Whitehead remarked that his doctrine "is entirely neutral on the question of immortality" in the subjective sense.[1] It is also true that in the *Dialogues*, Price quotes Whitehead as saying,

> "Insofar as man partakes of this creative process does he partake of the divine, of God, and that participation is his immortality, reducing the question of whether his individuality survives the death of the body to the estate of an irrelevancy."[2]

But as we shall see, a more positive view is possible.

Something of this sort does come under consideration by Professor Hartshorne. He accepts the Whiteheadian position that in the sense we have noted occasions never *wholly* perish and that they make their specific contribution to the ongoing process as this is gathered up in, and used by, God in the furthering of his purpose of shared good. He feels that there are no compelling philosophical arguments which would lead one to move on to, or on the other hand to reject, the conception of subjective, or as he calls it "personal", immortality for men. But he is himself inclined to reject personal immortality on the ground that to wish for it is to indulge in a kind of selfishness which refuses to accept and rejoice in any accomplishment of goodness or truth or beauty unless "I" can have a personal share in its triumph. For Hartshorne, much of the usual argument for personal immortality seems to reduce to a sort of "dog-in-the-manger" attitude to the universe; and since

[1] *Religion in the Making*, p. 111.
[2] Lucien Price: *The Dialogues of Alfred North Whitehead*, pp. 370f. (Frederick Muller Ltd, London).

the basic drive through the entire created order is un-
selfish action towards fuller good, this attitude appears
to him to be in flat contradiction to the purpose of
creation. The sheer fact of the achievement of the good,
linked as it is with the wonderful enrichment of the
divine experience through such achievement, ought to
be enough. The achievement is "for the greater glory
of God" as being himself supreme and all-inclusive love.
A man who sees this accomplished and delights in God's
"greater glory" should be sufficiently satisfied, Hartshorne thinks, without wishing that he himself "continue" and thus that he too may enjoy the beatitude
which has been achieved.

It seems to me that Hartshorne has here permitted
his justifiable dislike of certain popular ways of envisaging the possibility of immortality to dominate his thinking. The sort of approach which he condemns is indeed
self-centred to an unfortunate degree and may even be
said to be self-condemned. Yet there may be other ways of
thinking of immortality. May not "eternal life" provide a better conception? In any event, keeping entirely
on the level of speculative discussion, is it not possible
to follow consistently the line of thought advanced by
Whitehead and accepted by Hartshorne himself and
then go on to say something like the following?
Precisely because God is love and precisely because the
achievement of greater good, especially through the
activity of such personalized occasions as man may be
said to be, is in itself a good, may not the achieved good
include the agency *by which it was achieved*? May not
the satisfaction of the subjective aim which is specifically
human include as a necessary consequence some sort of
persistence of the creaturely agent, and cannot this

persistence itself enhance the ongoing process? Will not this in fact provide more ways in which the creative good can be both expressed and enjoyed?

This certainly should not mean a crudely individualistic notion of "glory for me", such as we associate with some sectarian Christian groups. It might very well suggest the rich conception of a "communion of saints" in which there is a joy that is shared in "widest commonalty", in and with God, as he rejoices in the growing good that thus becomes the further occasion for delight not only to himself but to other subjects of experience.

However this may be, it is apparent that there is not now, there never has been, and there never will be, any strictly logical demonstration of what the Christian is talking about when he speaks not so much of immortality as of "eternal life" and above all when he declares his faith in "resurrection". Process-thought, however, has made a very useful contribution by indicating that in one sense at least "there shall never be one lost good", since God accepts into himself, distils the worth or value from, and is able to use for his own loving purpose, every actual occasion in the created world. God participates intimately in his world and his world makes its contribution to God. This double movement delivers the creation from frustration and futility. Obviously (so I think) Christian faith must say something more; but the more that it says is not in contradiction to this conception of human and cosmic destiny. Rather it gives that conception an even fuller significance and a wider application.

Finally, what can be said of "the end of all things"? The insistence of process-thought on the ongoing movement of creativity, with the new emergent occasions and

the accomplishment of good in every part of the world
in spite of (and even in a way because of) the lags, the
backwaters, and the maladjustments, would suggest that
there is in fact *no* end. As it is the nature of God to be
creative and as it is the nature of the world to offer a
creative possibility for the Divine Activity, we may
conclude that for process-thinkers to speak of an "end",
in the chronological sense, would be to deny the very
presuppositions from which they start. But that *this*
epoch—this particular given process known to us in its
particular configurations—will come to an end would
seem indeed to be highly likely. If and when this particular epoch has reached its conclusion, with all the
good extracted from it that a living and loving God can
put into it and get out of it, we might well envisage other
epochs in which other kinds of good are to be achieved.
All this, however, is in the nature of sheer speculation.
What we know here is the "increasing purpose" which
runs through our epoch; we may rightly presume that
this purpose is the same as that which will run through
any and every epoch which could or which may appear.
For God *is* God, whatever his particular activity in this
or that place and time, or epoch, may be. To say that
God is God is to say that he is always active, living,
"moving out" to express his nature, rejoicing in every
expression of it, tenderly and compassionately entering
into relationship with every finite occasion to give it a
similar joy in actualizing all that may possibly be available for it, and accepting into himself all that is achieved
in the world. If something like this may legitimately be
asserted on the basis of a philosophical world-view such
as process-thought has developed, we have reason to be
grateful. If we are Christians, we have reason to think

that such assertions have a very important bearing on the validity of the faith by which we live: that God is indeed Love and that he has manifested this love in Jesus Christ, to the end that we may live through him.

B

In these lectures we have been attempting a presentation of some of the major assertions of contemporary process-philosophy which have particular relevance for Christian faith. Our presentation has sought to be objective, so far as this was possible; at any rate no effort has been made to twist these assertions in a specifically Christian direction. Our concern has been simply to indicate what process-thought in a general way has to tell us about God, the world, the nature of man and society, coupled with some discussion of its references to the historical figure of Jesus and its way of envisaging the destiny of man both in and beyond his present mortal existence. It has been our contention, however, that this way of looking at things is of special interest to the Christian theologian; and now and again this has been noted in the context of some given assertion of process-thought. In concluding the lectures, I should like to suggest that process-thought requires supplementation from at least three other areas of contemporary study and to urge that this supplementation will make it even more interesting to Christian thinkers.

First, I believe that it must be related to the existentialist outlook which is so prominent today both in Europe and in North and South America. Here I have especially in mind the insistence of existentialism on the involvement of the self in every interpretation of the meaning of the world, a point with which existentialist thinkers from Kierkegaard to Jaspers, Marcel, Sartre, and Heidegger have been much concerned. We have all come to see that theoretical detachment or the attempt at that sort of "objectivity" which includes *no* personal commitment is not in fact possible for man in any of the ultimate situations of life. Now this necessity for commitment is in no way alien to the general line taken in process-thought. Professor Hartshorne, for example, in a notable essay[1] has shown that there are many points of similarity between the thought of Whitehead and that of N. Berdyaev, the Russian existentialist thinker of the period between the two great wars. Furthermore, it can be shown, I think, that the insistence of process-thinkers on the "aesthetic" aspect in the world and in human experience, as well as the stress they put on the place of "decision" (at all levels from the sub-atomic to the human and divine) in bringing into actuality the various conceptual possibilities available for the world, represents a sort of metaphysical grounding for the more experiential insistence of the existentialists to whom we have referred. Teilhard is interesting here, with his talk of the "outside" and the "inside" of events. The importance in process-thought of inter-relationship and participation—or an organic and societal view—is another indication of similarity of outlook, for existentialism today (as in Heidegger) is emphatic on the "with-world" of our experience. We may conclude that in any use which is made of process-thought by Christian thinkers, due recognition must be given to the centrality

[1] In the American *Journal of Religion*, April 1957.

of commitment for a viable statement of the meaning of man's existence and the significance of the world of nature and history in which that existence occurs. Existentialist ideas are so well-known today that we need not dwell longer on this first point.

But the second emphasis, again one with which process-thought has many points of contact, will require longer discussion. I am now referring to the newer ways of understanding the meaning of history. There was a time when history was regarded as a cold and detached recording of events in the past; the job of the historian was to discover, so far as possible, "what had happened" and then to set this down in an appropriate series of entries in what really amounted to a kind of account-book. Today we find, however, that the nature of history is interpreted very differently indeed. History is no longer understood as a collection of dates, a dry series of chronicles; it is "the story of how we got this way", as I have often quoted from my old teacher Professor Frank Gavin. It is an entrance into the past, a re-living of the past, an imaginative participation in all the occurrences which have brought a given group or society, a given nation or culture, even the whole human race, to the place in which it now stands.

Still more interesting is the fairly recent discussion of the meaning of history which has pointed to something very like the ancient Jewish idea of "remembrance". We have known for a long time that the ancient Israelite believed that through certain actions or rites he was able to be present at, and actually share in, the events of the past which had created his people's life and thus had made him what as a member of that nation he was: a man who belonged to "the chosen people of God".

Thus at the annual Passover meal, for example, he did
not simply join with his family to "look back" at the
deliverance of the Jews from the hands of the Egyptians,
with all that this may have involved as a matter of
chronological record. Rather, at that meal he himself,
as a member of the Jewish people, was being delivered
afresh and was made a living participant in the event
in the past which, as he understood it, God had wrought
for his people. Much contemporary treatment of history
has put just such an emphasis on *anamnesis*; much is
said about the vital entrance of the historian into the
past, a participation which has the effect of making that
past come alive again in the present. This is not taken
to mean that the historian need not at all concern himself with what were actually the facts as they occurred.
He must endeavour to discover, so far as this is possible,
the precise way in which those events in the past did
take place. But the events are never "bare" events; they
always have a meaning. Hence once he has recovered
the events, the real historian must himself seek to enter
into and live through those events, and in his writing
about them he must seek continually to relate the meaning which they contain to the life of those who followed
and indeed to man's continuing experience up to the
present day.

Furthermore, the contemporary historian is aware,
as never before have historians been, of the remarkably
complex nature of historical events. Indeed he may
be said to share something of the process-thinker's view
that events are organic societies. No event has occurred
in isolation. The sound historian must take account of
what went before the event, of what was environmental
to the event, of what was consequent upon the event. All

this enters into the constantly expanding historical picture. It is impossible to understand in a serious fashion a specific historical occurrence—say, the Norman Conquest of 1066 or the American Revolution of the 1770's —without the fullest awareness of the rich variety of contributory factors which provided the preparation for, were related to, and resulted from this or that particular or "dated" moment or happening. This is why the historian's job is never completely finished and why new insight into historical events is continually leading to the writing of new "history". Once again, we are coming to see that events, in their remarkable richness, are societal in still another sense. Man is a "social animal" and what happens takes place in his social situation, with his fellows. Nothing in the realm of history happens to man as a "rugged individual", for no man is ever that. But it is also the case that events have a natural setting; there is, so to say, a geography of events. This cannot be neglected by the historian. Historical occurrences do not appear like the acting out of a drama on the neutral stage of nature, whatever certain recent biblical theologians may have seemed to suggest to the contrary. History and nature, nature and history, are inter-related most intimately and directly; and although much may be wrong with Professor Toynbee's discussion of history, he is surely right in insisting that climate, situation, and natural phenomena in all their great variety have played a genuine role in what he describes as the "challenge-and-response" theme which for him is the basic historical motif. It is hardly necessary to point out how all this is intimately related to the general position which, as we have seen, is adopted by process-thinkers.

Finally, as a third field of study with which process-thought must be related, I mention the new psychologies stemming from the work of Freud and Jung. Here I venture on a more detailed consideration, because these psychologies, despite their present differences and disagreements, have opened up to us a whole new dimension of experience and understanding which has to do with the profound depths of human existence in its emotional, valuational, conational, and intellectual aspects. We know a good deal more today about "what is in man" than we could claim to know half or even a quarter of a century ago. We have a better grasp of human motivations, the complex nature of human emotions, the development of personality and its dynamics, and the like. This new knowledge can be very disturbing, since it will not permit us to rest in older judgemental attitudes and demands of us new ways of evaluating the actions which spring from and are related to these startling "depths" in each human life.

Yet it is clear that any attempt to speak meaningfully of man and his place in the world must take this new material most seriously into the reckoning. And here again we find striking similarities with certain aspects of process-thought, especially in the stress which we have noted on "feeling-tones" and on the aesthetic element both in our experience and in the world at large. Furthermore, the portrayal in process-thought of man as an organism, inclusive of mental and emotional as well as physiological functioning, has a close relationship to the psychosomatic picture of man universally held by modern psychologists. It is impossible here to develop this theme more fully, nor is the lecturer competent to make the attempt; but we know that quite revolutionary changes in our traditional notions about human behaviour have already taken place and even more revolutionary changes are likely to take place when the discoveries of depth-psychology and psycho-somatics have been given their proper recognition.

As a single example, we may mention one area which is already undergoing change. I refer to the meaning and *modus operandi* of man's sexuality, to which we referred briefly in our last lecture. Our understanding of sex in the narrower sense of genital activity and in the wider sense of relationship with others has been so altered in recent years that the assumed fixity of thought in this area, with reference to auto-erotism, homo-erotism, and hetero-erotism, along with the related fixity which has been traditionally accepted in respect to judgements upon the right or wrong ways of sexual expression, has been shown to be indefensible by any intelligent standards. In consequence we find ourselves in a period of great fluidity in our understanding of moral criteria and their reference to man's sexual life.

We have already discussed in our last lecture the emergent nature of man, the meaning of his subjective aim, and his intended destiny in terms of his self-realization under the loving action of God—all this as understood in process-thought. A few comments may now be made about moral standards, as depth psychology illuminates that process portrayal of man; and our illustration, as we have indicated, will be from the area of man's sexual expression.

The conception of God as primarily loving creative activity, so strongly emphasized in process-thought, fits in admirably with the dominant motif of much that psychology tells us about *man's* sexual drive. If God is love, and has demonstrated this by his loving action in

the world, the responsive action of men is also characterized by love. This love is indeed a response to God,
but it is expressed not only and perhaps not chiefly
directly towards him, but in human relations with fellow-
men. Such relations have of necessity a sexual quality;
this is made abundantly clear by psychological study.

The emphasis on love, with its sexual overtones, does
not rule out the usefulness of moral law, but it most
emphatically restricts such law to the role of guidelines
or to a generally agreed consensus on ways in which love
may best be expressed in human behaviour and human
relations. When one couples this with what we have
said earlier about man's freedom, the openness to the
future which is before each of us and all of us, and the
importance of decision as to choices made, the moral
question is radically transformed from obedience to
arbitrary command to willing acceptance of the invita-
tion of love. In other words, much that is said by the
so-called "new morality", so much denigrated by tradi-
tionalists, is closer to the facts about man in his actual
human and cosmic situation than a morality which is
essentially restrictive and negative. Recent writers on
"situational ethics" and "contextual ethics" seem to have
understood this; and we are much indebted to them for
taking the first step in a reconception of the meaning of
morality, a task which is as important and necessary as
the reconception of Christian theology.

As we have said, it is very likely that the area of sexual
morality is central here, not only because it has to do
with a problem of such striking contemporary relevance
but because it follows from the significant role which
sexuality plays in the total pattern of human life. We
have noted that we are witnessing today a violent revul-

sion from traditional sexual morality which it is felt did not do justice to the nature of man. It is inevitable that there will be confusion and uncertainty, perhaps for a number of years, before some agreement can be reached on what should replace that older morality. The meaning of sexual relations, within and outside marriage, as well as more unusual sexual attitudes and behaviour, like homosexuality, will need to be reconsidered. What will be the final conclusion is by no means clear as yet. However, some points seem already to be obvious. The human expression of sexuality is always indicative of the personal quality of those who engage in such activity; and sexual acts which help to develop genuine personal life, but without destroying or damaging healthy human social relationships, must be evaluated in terms of the tenderness, mutuality, and faithfulness they display, even if they may seem to violate some inherited code. Such codes, like the Sabbath, were made for man, not man for the codes; and the final criterion of "rightness" must be the degree to which sexual self-expression in mutuality can play its part in freeing man from bondage to that which holds back or prevents his movement to realize the subjective aim of full manhood. Certainly in this context the family is always to be regarded as a means for the enhancing and not the restricting of human personality-in-relationship.

In other areas of human behaviour, similar principles are beginning to emerge. The "welfare state", for example, is an expression of a wide concern for love in relationship, but always with freedom guaranteed to the persons who constitute the society. In still another area, the treatment of criminals and the steps necessary to remove delinquency (perhaps especially among young people), we see once again an awakening of the spirit of loving understanding, with the intention of amelioration where there cannot be some prior averting of anti-social conduct. The role of punitive justice and retribution is more and more rejected. Here, as elsewhere, many will say that this means that modern society is removing all rules and becoming merely "permissive". But as we are taught by our deepening insight into the dominant role of love in the world and the central place of man's response to that love, and as a consequence of our better understanding of human nature in its psychological depths, we are beginning to see ever wider implications of the truth that God wills and works for men *to become men* and in freedom *to act like men*. This means to become and to act like God, who himself is love-in-action. The contribution of the psychological experts has been enormous here, and any sound statement of the meaning of human life, like any implementation of that meaning in personal existence and in social relationships, must be influenced by this contribution.

As we now come to the end of these lectures, let me then reiterate my belief that Christian theologians who are prepared to use process-thought in the task of reconception of Christian faith are required also to give due recognition to the three emphases with which we have just been concerned: to existentialism, to history in its new meaning, and to the insights of modern psychological enquiry. Perhaps it is fair to say that as a matter of fact it has been the theologians who adopt an evolutionary perspective who have also been *most* inclined to welcome this newer knowledge, although it is of course true that theologians of other persuasions have also been prepared to employ (to a greater or less degree) the findings of one or other of those schools of thought.

What is needed today, I believe, is the radical attempt to work out a theological pattern for Christian faith which is in the main influenced by process-philosophy, while at the same time use is made of what we have been learning from the existentialist's insistence on engagement and decision, the understanding of history as involving genuine participation and social context, and the psychologist's awareness of the depths of human emotional, conational, and rational experience. It is to be hoped that those who engage in the task will remember that this attempt would necessarily be an *essay* in reconception, making no pretence to being conclusive or exhaustive. But a considerable number of such experiments would be of great value in furthering the perennial task of thinking-through once again what it means to "confess that Jesus Christ is Lord, to the glory of God the Father".

Now what *is* this Christian faith? Here we must acknowledge our indebtedness to the work of theologians like Karl Barth, Emil Brunner, and others of the so-called "neo-orthodox" reaction of the years 1930–50. Some of us—certainly I myself—feel that their position is disastrously one-sided and their dismissal of philosophy incredibly narrow. Yet we must admit that through their work we have learned to take very seriously the total biblical story, reading with deeper insight the truths which are there stated not in propositions but in the events of history and in the response made to those events in the experience of men and women immersed in the ordinary affairs of daily life. And again, through the work of other scholars like Bultmann and Buri, with their frank recognition of the mythological element in the biblical story, we have come to see that the affirmations of Scripture have their abiding significance, not in spite of, but precisely because of their being stated in language which can only be described as highly metaphorical. We have learned to read with sympathy and understanding the meaning that is in and behind the "myth". We cannot rest content with the myth itself, in its literal sense; but we can get at what the myth was saying, and saying in a manner appropriate to its time and place. We have come to see, as a matter of fact, that religious assertion by its very nature is inevitably couched in such metaphorical, symbolical, if you will poetical, language; and that all deep faith must express itself in this way if it is to express itself at all.

Thus we are prepared to grant that the Christian faith is told through a story or drama. It is a story that has to do with the human life of Jesus Christ, understood in the light of all that preceded and prepared for his appearance, and apprehended for what it really signified through an awareness of what followed upon it and was nourished and empowered by his appearance in history. This faith, which sees Jesus as revelation of God in action in history, rests upon the commitment of men to the life which the story unfolds, or rather, to the person of Jesus himself—grasped in the depths of each man's existence as being what Whitehead said it was: "the revelation of the nature of God and of his agency in the world".

The fact of Christ, thus known in total commitment, has led to a way of thinking, of feeling, of doing, of living, which is marked by his Spirit and informed by a sense of his continuing presence and power in the world.

The implications of this commitment in faith to fact, or (as we might say) in engagement of life with the historic, crucified, and "risen" Lord, have been worked out in Christian theology within the context of the communal life of the Christian fellowship and through the worship and obedience which are the expression of Christian discipleship. It is this faith which requires theological reconception in our own day; and some of us are convinced that process-thought, coupled with the other contributions to which I have referred, is most likely to help us in this task.

BIBLIOGRAPHY

Alexander, Samuel: *Space, Time and Deity*; Macmillan and Co., London, 1927.

Anshen, R. N. (Ed.): *Alfred North Whitehead: His Reflections on Nature and Man*; Harper and Row, New York, 1961.

Blamires, H. A.: *The Christian Mind*; S.P.C.K., London, 1963.

Buren, P. van: *The Secular Meaning of the Gospel*; S.C.M. Press, London, 1963.

de Chardin, P. Teilhard: *Le Milieu Divin*; Collins, London, 1960.
  The Future of Man; Collins, London, 1964.
  The Phenomenon of Man; Collins, London, 1961.

Cobb, John B. Jr.: *A Christian Natural Theology*; Westminster Press, Philadelphia, 1965.
  The Structure of Christian Experience; Westminster Press, Philadelphia, 1967; Lutterworth Press, London, 1968.

Hamilton, P. N.: *The Living God and the Modern World*; Hodder and Stoughton, London, 1967; United Church Press, Philadelphia, 1968.

Harris, E. E.: *Revelation through Reason*; Allen and Unwin, London, 1959.

Hartshorne, Charles: *The Divine Relativity*; Yale University Press, 1948.

The Logic of Perfection; Open Court Press, LaSalle, Ind., 1962.

A Natural Theology for Our Times; Open Court Press, LaSalle, Ind., 1967.

Reality as Social Process; Free Press, Glencoe, Illinois, 1953; Collier-Macmillan, New York, 1963.

Man's Vision of God; Harper and Brothers, New York, 1941.

Hartshorne, C. and Reese, W. L.: *Philosophers Speak of God*; University of Chicago Press, 1953.

Lyman, E. W.: *The Meaning and Truth of Religion*; Charles Scribner's Sons, New York, 1933.

Matthews, W. R.: *The Purpose of God*; James Nisbet and Co., 1935.

Leibrecht, W. (Ed.): *Religion and Culture: Essays in Honour of Paul Tillich*; Harper and Row, New York, and S.C.M. Press, London, 1959.

Morgan, C. Lloyd: *Emergent Evolution*; Henry Holt, New York, 1926.

Life, Mind and Spirit; Williams and Norgate, London.

Ogden, Schubert: *Christ Without Myth*; Harper and Row, New York, 1961; Collins, London, 1962.

The Reality of God; Harper and Row, New York, 1966, and S.C.M. Press, London, 1967.

Paton, H. J.: *The Modern Predicament*; Allen and Unwin, London, 1955.

Peters, F. H.: *The Creative Advance*; Bethany Press, St Louis, Mo., 1966.

Price, Lucien: *The Dialogues of Alfred North Whitehead*; Frederick Muller, London.

Robinson, J. A. T.: *Honest to God*; S.C.M. Press, London, 1963.

Sherburne, D. W.: *Whiteheadian Aesthetic*; Yale University Press, 1961.

Key to Whitehead's Process and Reality; Macmillan, New York, 1966.

Smuts, J. C.: *Holism and Evolution*; Macmillan and Co., London, 1936.

Stockwood, M. (Ed.): *Cambridge Sermons*; Faith Press, London, 1959; Hodder and Stoughton, London, 1961.

Thornton, L. S.: *The Incarnate Lord*; Longmans Green, London, 1928.

Tillich, Paul: *Systematic Theology*; James Nisbet and Co., Vol. I, 1953; Vol. II, 1957; Vol. III, 1964; One volume edition, 1968.

Whitehead, A. N.: *Adventures of Ideas*; Cambridge University Press, 1933.

Modes of Thought; Cambridge University Press, 1938.

Essays in Science and Philosophy; Rider and Co., London, 1948.

Process and Reality; Cambridge University Press, 1927.

Religion in the Making; Cambridge University Press, 1926.

Science and the Modern World; Cambridge University Press, 1936.

Symbolism: Meaning and Effect; Cambridge University Press, 1927.

Williams, D. D.: *The Spirit and the Forms of Love*; James Nisbet and Co., and Harper and Row, New York, 1968.